(1973)

12/3.

The
Corporate
Eunuch

The Corporate Eunuch

by
O. William Battalia
and
John J. Tarrant

Abelard-Schuman

To the college graduates of the 70s
. . . who in reaching their prime years
will be the managers and executives
who can help shape the face of tomorrow
as we cross into the twenty-first century

Abelard-Schuman Limited
450 Edgware Road   24 Market Square
London W2   Aylesbury, Bucks

Printed in Great Britain by
Billing & Sons Limited, Guildford and London

Introduction

Our society is a collection of pyramids, and we're all sentenced to serve time at some level in some pyramid. Trouble is the pyramids don't function very well, and most of the inmates are restless. It seems that the more money HEW spends, the less effect there is on the health, education and welfare of the people. The auto pyramids produce 12 million cars and have to recall 13 million. Worse, they've lost sight of their goal of safe, economical transportation; the bus and the rail are threats, not opportunities, and the auto must be sold at any social cost in lives and lungs. At the top of each pyramid, the manager feels impotent and his work seems purposeless; down the line, the work is boring and meaningless. Ecologists and consumerists, unable to effect change, are often settling for monkey wrenches in the machinery and sugar in the gas tanks. Meanwhile, Congress goes on operating as if under eight feet of warm peanut butter.

It may be that a transition period lies ahead. If so, chances are a lot of industries and activities will wither and disappear while new ones materialize. Let us pray that the new ones don't take pyramids for granted. In any case, in this kind of period, of necessity many people will be fired or will decide to look for new jobs.

This book should be a help to anybody who is worried about his or her work life. Which is not to say that I agree with everything in it. Chapter 11, "Breaking through the Confines of the Organization Chart," advises a newly promoted executive to hire a management consultant to help him learn his new job. Actually, all he has to do for a much better education is start visiting the people who report to him (and the people who report to them) and asking questions like: "What should we start doing around here?" and "What should we stop doing around here?" and "What's stopping you from being the best in the world at your work?" A month or so of listening to answers to questions

v

like that and the new executive will know which way excellence lies. I also heartily disagree with Chapter 13, The Problem of Visibility, which advocates turning yourself into a self-promoter. To me, this is like advising someone who is angry and frustrated to shoot up a little heroin: it may produce some short-term relief, but in the long run it will create more problems than it solves. At any rate, I think there is more than enough first-rate stuff in the book to make up for the dubious advice.

The main subject of the book is what goes on in the pyramids, and this is really top-drawer. When the authors get on to how-to-succeed-in-a-pyramid, they are less successful. With one exception: Chapter 15, "The Search for the Safe Plateau." Here we're told to defy the Peter Principle. When you find a job you enjoy doing and which pays enough to support your family, don't let yourself be promoted out of it. Biology teacher: don't become head of the Biology Department! Salesman: don't take that job as sales manager! Makes a lot of sense to me. Having found your niche, you grow more expert every year. With your expertise come security, satisfaction, and the power to get adequate tools for your people and your work, and to ward off unnecessary outside interference. Just make sure the tools you ask for are really needed, and that the outside threat is really uncalled for. Happiness through increasing expertise and the suppression of ambition! Pretty good.

From my own experience, there are four other ways you can cope with life in the pyramids.

1. *Drop Out.* Actual case: Al Hapke, born in St. Louis in 1908, lived on a Wisconsin farm, went to Yale on a swimming scholarship, class of 1933. Worked for the Herald Tribune, then W. R. Grace. After two years in the Navy as a pilot, he flew South American routes for PanAm. Test pilot for Bell Aircraft. Then to Republic Aviation as research manager on the P47 Thunderbolt. Helped reorganize the aircraft industry association, and then went to the American Petroleum Institute to set up their aviation policies. Back to Republic as European manager headquartered in Paris with

48 men in NATO countries selling the F105. Briefly with Lockheed heading sales of commercial products, and then set up a leasing and finance distributorship in California. That's a bunch of pyramids. In 1962, at age 54, he started building a sailboat to escape from the ratrace. Got fired by the finance company. Lived on unemployment insurance and odd jobs while completing boat which was launched in 1964. Lived aboard reading and buying books for the boat's library. Shoved off in December, 1965, with his wife, some cats, and $280. Sailed down around the tip of Baja and up into the Gulf of California. Lived there for four years fishing, reading and bartering English lessons for food. Came back, swapped the boat for a VW camper plus cash and has since been observing the state of the nation from the grass-roots level.

2. *Drop Out and Build Your Own Unpyramid.* Actual case: Don Dible, born 1936. After high school spent four years in the U.S. Air Force. Earned a B.S. in electrical engineering at M.I.T. and then an M.S. at Stanford. Worked for seven years for small electronics firms; held positions like manager of the engineering department and national sales manager. Decided to start own business. Attended seminars and read what he could find. Discovered there was no good comprehensive text but a lot of interest. Wrote *Up Your Own Organization.* Couldn't find a publisher, so he formed Entrepreneur Press, Santa Clara, California 95051 and published it himself in 1971. To date has sold 6000 copies at $25 each, recovering all his costs and making a modest profit. The book stimulated so much campus interest that he's bringing out a half-price edition for colleges and universities.

3. *Stay In but Stay Independent.* Find a company that pays you to do what you enjoy doing anyway. Live in a camper on as low a standard of living as you can. Don't buy a television set because it will up your consumption and lower your satisfaction. Live monogamously with the mate of your choice (hopefully your mate will want to work too) but don't get married. Above all, don't have any children, for that leads to the house and appliances and installment

credit and dependence on that particular job in that particular pyramid. Bank all your excess earnings. Then if the company gives you an impossible boss or shifts you to work you don't enjoy, you can unplug the camper, give them all the cheery finger, and live on your bank account while you and your campermate look for more satisfying work. If you find your safe plateau, *then* get married, buy your TV, have your children and became part of the problem.

4. *Become a Leader.* If you are man enough (or woman enough), try to become a leader. With a little luck, you'll get a new managerial assignment and that's the time to start. Suppress your own ego and your own ambition. Think only of your people and what they're supposed to do for the organization. Help them get the tools they need; help them over the obstacles. When something goes wrong you take the blame. When a success comes along see that you don't take any credit but pass it all down. [It always works. Wouldn't you work harder and smarter for a boss like that than for the boss you've got?] When your part of the pyramid begins to attract attention for its excellence, don't let the bosses get away with just giving *you* a raise. It's your people who deserve the money, and if you're fighting nonsense and injustice you won't let any salary gaps open up between you and your people. After all, why should you be paid so much? As leader (contrast with manager) you're really only the servant of your people. Anybody can be a good servant. Nader is a good leader. Think how he operates. How long would he last if he moved all his groups into the Nader Building, lived in a penthouse, came to the office in a limousine, and smoked big fat cigars?

When you lead (serve) instead of manage, your people will do better. You will enjoy doing it, but eventually you will be noticed and promoted. Then do it again. I started as a security analyst and wound up as a chief executive that way. With some luck.

Good luck to you whichever way you go.

And peace to those who deserve it.

Robert Townsend

Preface

This book is about the American corporate manager who has made it many rungs up the success ladder, who has achieved a position in which he has status, money and power, but who still feels restless and unfulfilled. This book is about how to make a success of *success*.

To a great extent men and women succeed in management because they put a major proportion of their life's energy into their careers. To this driving commitment they harness superb skills that have made American scientific management a dominant force in the world. Their lives are inextricably linked with their work.

It is futile to tell such people that they should not take their jobs so seriously, that they should merely do an uninvolved day's work in the office, but really *live* away from it. The job of management takes more than this. It can be much, even all, of their lives.

In this book we talk about how a good manager can find more fulfillment and be more productive on the job. We reveal how the manager can move to another job that is not just a change of scene, but a new way of management life. We examine the factors that can make managers uneasy and tense about their jobs even when they do them well.

We also pinpoint the trends that cause ever-increasing restlessness in the executive suite and we offer specific plans and recommendations that provide for greater career fulfillment through more effective operation. We take a hard look at the balance between office and home. We suggest ways in which the manager can give

Preface

his professional life all the energy and attention it requires, and still be a successful husband and father.

No book can be a panacea. Based upon our years of observation and research into the nature of executive responsibility and the pressures that it entails, this book can help you if:

You believe that you are not managing up to your full potential

You think longingly, on occasion, on getting out of the rat race

You would like to move to a better-paying and more satisfying job

You are convinced that your progress up the corporate ladder has not brought you everything you hoped it would

Such feelings torment more and more managers each day. From their experiences, you can come to a better understanding of what is happening—and what you can do about it.

Acknowledgments

Special mention and grateful acknowledgment should be paid to Mr. R. James Lotz, Jr., partner in the firm of Battalia, Lotz and Associates, Inc. During the book's preparation, he was an inspired influence in its development and in our thinking.

Also, many clients that have worked with through the years deserve special mention, but many of them are not in a position to be identified directly with the viewpoints expressed in this book.

Contents

1/
The Emasculation of the Manager   1

2/
The New Religion of Management   10

3/
The Concept of the Disposable Manager   19

4/
What the Corporate Eunuch Has Going for Him—and
    Against Him   32

5/
The Hole in the Busy Day   40

6/
The Endless Business Conference   48

7/
Should Managers Be Married?   61

8/
I'll Go into Business for Myself   73

9/
The Executive Emporium   83

10/
How to Manage Success   98

11/
Breaking Through the Confines of the Organization Chart   109

12/
Delegate to Suit Yourself   124

13/
The Problem of Visibility   135

Contents

14/
Playing the Corporate Field   146

15/
The Search for the Safe Plateau   155

16/
How to Win by Losing   166

17/
Manager, Manage Thyself   173

The Emasculation of the Manager / 1

On or off the job, nobody seems to like the American manager anymore, and he is reminded of this melancholy fact all day long.

8:30 A.M. The manager unfolds his newspaper. Headlines strike his eye: NADER ACCUSES TOP BRASS. . . . TAX PLAN TO HIT 'RICH.'

9:30 A.M. The manager enters his office building, passing pickets whose signs proclaim that his company is helping to kill women and children in Southeast Asia.

10:00 A.M. At a conference the manager begins to make suggestions about solving a corporate problem. A colleague cuts in to say that they've heard all that before, what they need is fresh thinking.

11:00 A.M. The manager reads a letter from a government agency. His operation is polluting the water and air. What is he going to do about it?

12:30 P.M. Since part of the manager's job is to try to recruit promising university graduates, he takes a young man to lunch. The young man declares, "A business career is not for me. I want to do something significant with my life."

3:00 P.M. A production-line supervisor comes into the manager's office with a grievance. The manager remarks that they have known each other for many years and have always gotten along all right. If he can possibly do something for the supervisor, he will. The blue-collar man doesn't buy it: "You sit here behind a big desk in an air-conditioned office. You don't know what's going on."

4:30 P.M. The manager reluctantly informs a long-time subordinate that his request for a raise did not go through. The subordinate says, "Yeah, what the hell do you care? You've got it made."

5:15 P.M. The manager looks for a file his new secretary was supposed to get for him before she went home. It's not there. His old secretary would have done it, but she left three months ago to join a commune.

6:40 P.M. As he drives home from the station, the manager has to brake sharply as a sleek, souped-up sports car cuts in front of him. From the bearded driver of the sports car the manager receives a one-finger salute.

7:15 P.M. The manager asks his son why he is cutting high-school classes. His son replies, "All you care about is me getting good marks and going to college and turning out like you. You don't understand what I want at all."

8:45 P.M. The manager attends a community meeting. Some people want to change the zoning laws in his town to permit low-income housing. A black leader from a nearby city tells the manager and his neighbors, "You fat cats are through keeping us in our place. We're coming whether you like it or not!"

11:30 P.M. Not ready for sleep, the manager turns

on a TV talk show. He watches while Gloria Steinem tells him that he owes his wife at least $8,000 per year in back pay for regular housekeeping chores, "not including part-time prostitution privileges."

12:15 P.M. The manager goes to bed. He is still not sleepy. He reaches out to his wife, who says she is too tired and she will see him in the morning. He reflects that at least he is no longer incurring liabilities for prostitution privileges.

Normally, all of this might be bearable. The man on top has never been too popular in our society. And after all, the executive who climbs a significant part of the way up the corporate ladder has a number of very strong plus factors going for him. He is well paid. He has power. And, at least within his own corporate world, he has status.

But something else is happening to the American manager. To a far greater extent than ever before, he does not like himself. He questions the meaning of his life. He looks into the future, and he does not care much for what he sees.

He is tired of fighting his way upstream. He longs to find a quiet pool in which he can swim in peace. He dreams of dropping out of the rat race with security, honor and his wits about him. But he has obligations, reservations and fears. He would like to drop out, but not all the way.

There are ways in which he can do this. To understand how they work, we must first examine the path along which the manager has come to reach his present dubious eminence.

In the first half of the twentieth century, American management planning, thinking, innovation and execution became the envy of the world. To Jean Jacques Servan-Schreiber, a leader of France's Radical Socialist Party and author of *The American Challenge*, the key to American domination was the skill and drive of its management class, not the country's resources or its population. And it was this very skill and drive which Servan-Schreiber and many others like him urged Europe to emulate. The American businessman built a country and a society, and he seemed to have made himself happy doing it.

But today's executive is different from the American manager of a former day. It goes beyond just wearing his hair a little longer or his suits wider at the lapels. Beyond operating in a more complex economy or a more sophisticated marketplace. Nor is the difference a matter of education or values.

The fundamental nature of managership has radically changed. This has had a profound effect upon managers, and the effect has not been good. The skills of craftsmanship and the skills of personal understanding have been replaced by the skills of communication and the skills of administration. Concreteness has given way to abstraction, things to symbols. Fulfillment has been replaced by emptiness. Today many highly successful, highly gifted men feel unfulfilled, dissatisfied, hollow.

Some try to ease the feeling of emptiness through mobility. Battalia, Lotz and Associates conducted a confidential survey of upper-level managers which showed that the average length of their careers was 19 years: the average number of job changes was four, with approximately 4.75 years per job. Henry K. Astwood of the Sales Manpower Foundation, a job clearinghouse for salesmen and sales executives, concurs: he finds the average job tenure of the marketing executives who pass through his institution to be about 4.5 years. And of course, except when the economy is tight, this sort of mobility is highly possible for an executive, for we are in the day of the interchangeable manager.

Under the influential sponsorship of the American Management Association, the idea has grown that a good executive need not be very familiar with the nitty-gritty of what a company makes and sells. According to the AMA, there are only four things that a gifted manager, moving into a top policy-making job, has to know about his new organization: its legal position, its philosophy, its long-range goals and its budget. Thus a good man can move from the shoe business to the turbine business to the chewing-gum business. We see examples of this sort of interindustry mobility in the financial pages every day.

Of course this was not always the case. In a special supplement to the *New York Times,* November 19, 1967, the Sales Executives Club of New York proudly explained how the current situation has come about, "The marketing revolution has been happening for more than a century—but in the last few years it has gained impetus. To see what has happened to marketing, let's trace the history of a fictitious company—J. M. Ramsey, Inc."

The story begins with the founding of the Ramsey company a hundred years ago when John Ramsey set up his forge in a little village on the banks of the Ohio River. He made, repaired and sold farm implements to

5

his neighbors. He did a good job, charged honest prices and was proud of it. His was an *owner-oriented* enterprise.

As John Ramsey's business grew, he came to a conclusion: he could sell more by going to potential customers than by waiting until they came to his shop. He couldn't go in person because someone had to take care of the store. So Ramsey began to build a sales force. He was proud of the implements he made. He expected his salesmen to sell them. If not, he got other salesmen. In this phase the company was *manufacturing oriented.*

The years went on. John Ramsey's son became more active in the running of the business, and he talked about it in a different way, "We're a farm-implement company, we make quality merchandise—and we think it's the best available. We have built a top-flight sales organization to sell what we make at a favorable price and we will do everything within reason to support that sales organization and keep it a strong one." During this period the company was *sales oriented.*

Through the early decades of the twentieth century, the Ramsey Corporation grew and spread out. It went public. It set up branches for national distribution, but essentially the company continued to make a single line of high-quality products and sell them. However, World War II brought product diversification. As peace returned, the company used its wartime experience to make a diversity of products. John Ramsey III declared, "Ramsey makes products for consumers of various kinds all over the world. We have to know what the consumer wants and reach him with it at the right time and the right price. To do this, we must coordinate a number of functions: selling; advertising; research; product planning; manufacturing; and finance." At this time the company was *marketing oriented.*

The Ramsey Corporation continued to change and grow. It moved to a stage at which its philosophy was articulated this way: "Our responsibility is to use all of our skills to serve our many owners, our millions of customers and the society we live in. We can accomplish this by proceeding on the assumption that every activity of the company, without exception, is designed to satisfy public need at a profit to our company." At this point the Ramsey Corporation was *consumer oriented.*

This supplement was published in 1967. Since then, oddly enough, we might well imagine the Ramsey Corporation coming full circle back to *owner orientation.* It may have become a gigantic conglomerate encompassing a bizarre diversity of acquired companies and enterprises which have no unifying factor, except that someone thought each division capable of contributing a profit, or in some cases an advantageous tax loss, to the stockholders.

Whether or not this is the case, we have certainly come a long way from old John Ramsey, who made farm implements and was proud of them. This is the road that American industry has traveled. Along the road the edifices have become bigger and grander and the dwellings richer and more lavish. The men walking that road are far better off than their counterparts of a hundred years ago. So why do they look so unhappy?

They can move from one Ramsey-like corporation to another, but they can't hide. And when, as recently, a financial pinch comes along, many managers find that *interchangeable* can be a synonym for *disposable.*

In our view, the pendulum has swung too far in the

direction of the interchangeable manager. Our experience leads us to believe that the man with a gut feeling for the enterprise does have an advantage over his counterpart who can only channel and administer. But at the moment we are talking only of how the man in the job feels. In many ways he doesn't feel so good. He talks but does not do. He deals in the obscure. He worries about his job because there is no sure way to gauge the qualities the job requires, and so there is no way to tell whether he is better at his job than somebody else would be. And there are a dozen somebody elses who want the job.

Naturally he is very busy. He examines mathematical models. He reads research reports. He eyes flow charts. He runs meetings. He attends seminars. He generates projections. He plans strategies. He formulates budgets. And yet some days he does not really feel that he has accomplished a damn thing, and he feels that he is not accomplishing much at home either. His skills are becoming like those of the experts who inscribe the Lord's Prayer on the head of a pin—interesting and demanding—but what good is it?

Still, it is absolutely necessary for the manager to maintain a facade and a steady flow of articulate self-confidence. The firm jaw, the crisp collar, the taut crease, the decisive, forceful finger on the telephone dial. He must be in uniform and in character at all times, ready for the cry, This looks like a job for Management Man!

The role of the management man has always been a demanding one. It is becoming more and more dissatisfying; in fact, managership is depleting to the point of emasculation.

If this were all that could be said about modern,

high-pressure management—that it emasculates the individual who labors under its burdens—many managers might choose a more wholesome and happier way of life, but perhaps just as many others would feel that in spite of everything, the rewards and accomplishments outweigh the hazards. But the indictment is more comprehensive than this. Until recently, the modern method of management has always been highly effective in getting things done and in building profitable careers for those who practice it. But things are changing.

There are deep and sweeping movements in business today which are making it increasingly difficult for the management man to be as effective as he was a few years ago. We are plainly about to see a return to older and, in some cases, discredited methods of running a business operation. In the course of this reversion, life will become simpler, more healthy and more satisfying for management practitioners who are astute enough to see and grasp the trend.

The New Religion
of Management/2

An interesting thing happened to the manager in 1954. He became a god.

Such an occurrence is always initially pleasurable to the object of the divine elevation, but things do not always remain in that happy state. As Sir James Frazer pointed out in *The Golden Bough,* the lot of the divinity is not always a pleasant one. Among many peoples of the ancient world, it was customary to elevate individuals to divine status. But the exalted position was rarely a permanent one. Often divinities were for worship until the harvest was brought in—then they were for killing in ritual sacrifice.

Of course it would be different if the manager had been made a god in the Judeo-Christian tradition—all-seeing, omnipotent, eternal. But the life of the management god is more like those of the Roman and Greek gods—full of pleasant and unpleasant surprises, anxiety and conflict.

The prime mover in making a religion of management—and the apotheosis of the manager—is Peter Drucker, a Viennese-born economist, writer and consultant to American business. When Drucker established his religion, as is so often the case, he also established himself its chief prophet. And Drucker has shown remarkable endurance in this role. Presidents, most recently Mr. Nixon, have asked Mr. Drucker's advice and issued tributes to his omniscience. Even *New York Magazine,* the sophisticated Manhattan publication, recognizes his preeminence. In its January 17, 1972, issue, the magazine editorially noted the article by management consultant Alan Lakein on the use of time: "Peter Drucker, author of *The Effective Executive,* is the foremost man in his particular area, and Lakein enthusiastically acknowledges his intellectual debt to Drucker."

In 1954, Peter Drucker published *The Practice of Management.* The book's subtitle, *A Study of the Most Important Function in American Society,* sets the tone. Many executives and businessmen have read *The Practice of Management,* many more have not. However, they all function in the atmosphere the book has helped create.

Its theme is established in the initial sentence: "The manager is the dynamic, life-giving element in every business." And in this role the manager's activities have ramifications far beyond the office walls, since "management will remain a basic and dominant institution perhaps as long as western civilization itself survives." Drucker goes on to preach the mystique of modern scientific management.

This is not to be confused with the scientific management movement which grew out of the experiments of Frederick W. Taylor in the 1880s and which flourished around the turn of the century. Taylor's thesis was that

11

the manager is responsible for defining the task which the worker is to perform, selecting the proper worker for the job, and motivating the worker to a high level of performance. When managers properly perform these tasks, Taylor maintained, efficiency increases.

These were once revolutionary ideas, but they have now fallen into disfavor. In *Managerial Psychology,* published by the University of Chicago Press in 1958, Harold J. Leavitt, professor of industrial administration and psychology at Carnegie Tech, tells us why. "Though Taylor worried empirically about the layout of jobs and the physiological capacities of individuals, he did not pay much attention to people's psyches." The idea is, management is far more mysterious and transcendental than anything ever dreamed of in Frederick Taylor's philosophy. The manager is not just a boss. He does not just tell people what to do.

In the Druckerian creed, what does the manager do? Page 341 of *The Practice of Management* tells us the manager has two specific tasks. First, "the manager has the task of creating a true whole that is larger than the sum of its parts, a productive entity that turns out more than the sum of the resources put into it." The manager's second specific task "is to harmonize in every decision and action the requirements of the immediate and long-range future." These tasks, of course, are somewhat vague, just as the precepts of a new religion so often are. The question is, how does the manager behave in the fulfillment of these tasks? What does he do?

Drucker lays out five basic operations. A manager *sets objectives.* A manager *organizes.* A manager *motivates and communicates.* A manager *establishes measuring yardsticks.* A manager *develops people.* From,

12

through, and around the ramifications of these basics has come the phenomenon of managership with which we are concerned today.

As is the case with any developing discipline (or for that matter, religion), the modern art of management has provided a fertile field for theorists and innovators of all sorts. Management thinkers—many of them industrial psychologists—have been a constant source of new concepts, new formulations, new nostrums, all ostensibly designed to make the bewilderingly complex task of management possible, or at least acceptable, for the individual who must practice it. Thus down the years we have had a succession of such terms as brainstorming, the management grid, Theory X and Theory Y, sensitivity training, management by objectives (MBO), organizational development (OD). At any given time in the comfortable surroundings of Cambridge or Westchester or Aspen, Colorado, there will be groups of middle to upper level executives discussing these things.

Somehow new terms achieve overnight popularity at such gatherings and then subside into disuse. For example, it has recently become almost a badge of status for the executive to talk about trade-offs: data processing trade-offs between terminal accessibility and data shelf-life, trade-offs between debt and equity, and so on. Some observers who attend high-level conferences at which the latest concepts are discussed in the newest terms may be struck by an interesting fact. Most of those participating in the discussion do not really know what they are talking about.

This in no way demeans the intelligence, competence or literacy of the managers involved. The point is that their tutors, the management philosophers who bring these terms to prominence and popularity, are often either so vague or so impenetrable that their real meaning cannot be detected. This is partly protective. In any discipline the man who comes up with a new concept or a new approach to things first surrounds the concept with a defensive network of jargon. While this makes it difficult for rivals to steal the idea, it also makes it equally difficult for anyone else to grasp the idea too readily. If this is not done—if the concept is instead transmitted in plain English—there is real danger that the acolyte will quickly see the whole thing (the Gestalt) and exclaim, "But that's just common sense!" Worse, he might even observe that the emperor has no clothes on and cry out, "But that doesn't mean anything!" The latter reaction is of course worse than the former, but neither is welcomed by the progenitor of a new management concept.

So management man must be up on all the latest terms and be abreast of all the newest enthusiasms. When someone uses the latest catch phrase over the lunchtable or at a conference, he must recognize it and be able to respond in kind. However, response need not imply understanding.

Most managers who have day-in, day-out jobs to perform make a conscientious effort to understand new management concepts and to translate them into tools that help to get the job done. The pure prophets of management often deplore a good number of these mundane executive activities. Drucker tells us, "Every manager does many things that are not managing." Here he means that a sales manager may make a statistical analysis of the market, a manufacturing manager may design a new plant, or a company president may nego-

14

tiate a large bank loan. These things are necessary, Drucker and his followers admit, but they are not managing.

The trouble is that many executives will not or cannot draw the distinction between those things which are managing and those things which are not. They have jobs to do, they look to management theorists for help in doing those jobs, and so they translate the utterances of the theorists into everyday, common-sense language.

This does not always work out so well. One example may be found in sensitivity training. The advocates of sensitivity training, notably Chris Argyris of Yale, have mounted a rather complex method of getting managers better attuned to the many variations of human behavior. They have stressed the subtlety of the technique, and they have underscored the importance of professional guidance. Nevertheless, a lot of working managers have considered what they have heard and read about sensitivity training and have quite understandably concluded that all they have to do is get a bunch of people in a room and let their hair down to the point where each one tells the other guy exactly what he thinks of him.

In some organizations this simplification has been played out with disastrous results. One president took his five key division heads out on his yacht for an afternoon of sensitivity training on Long Island Sound. Within a week one man had resigned. A month later another took early retirement. It was three months before any of the participants spoke to one another except in the line of duty. The company has yet to recover from the excursion.

When management by objectives came along, it was

seized upon by hard-pressed executives as a good notion that was bound to make a tough job a lot easier. In effect, MBO became management by results. In application this means that you give a subordinate a job to do, lay out his objectives and then forget about it. Six months or a year later, he has either delivered or he has not. Granted, this is a distortion of the concept as formulated by the coiners of MBO, but it is a natural and understandable distortion.

Just one of the results of this application, as noted by Norman Jaspan, the expert on business security and loss prevention, has been a great increase in high-level business crime. It is not just that the opportunity for embezzlement is greater. The harried executive, knowing that he is to be judged only by results, finds himself increasingly forced into a position where he juggles figures and inventories to produce those results. Even worse, the practice of setting objectives for subordinates and then forgetting about them gives some top-level executives a temporary opportunity to sleep better off nights, but in the end it fails to produce significantly better results. Indeed the harvest is often calamitous. Perhaps worst of all is the thought that if the only thing the top-level executive must do is set objectives, he can very easily be replaced by a computer.

Organizational development is a more recent enthusiasm. Many refinements in management methods—some useful, some not—have marched under the banner of OD. But what does organizational development mean? This question was asked recently of a number of executives who had just spent three days discussing the topic under the aegis of the American Management

16

Association. None could come up with an adequate answer.

Realizing the nebulous form which this attractive concept seems to take at the operating level, certain management philosophers have adopted a most imaginative means of rationalization. Writing in *Harvard Business Review*, Edgar F. Huse and Michael Beer place their stamp of approval on the "eclectic approach to organizational development." They recognize that "many executives have come to equate organizational development with this technique or that one, and if the method is one they feel uncomfortable with, they may think they have to reject the whole concept." The line taken by Messrs. Huse and Beer is to study the application of organizational development in various departments of a single business. In one department, productivity was increased through job enrichment; in another, the answer was to organize the workers into teams. In a third operation, management structured a department along organization product lines, replacing a more specialized setup. In still another department, a supervisor achieved better performance by instilling trust.

At first glance these various techniques do not seem to have much in common. However, Huse and Beer assure their readers that all may be grouped under the general heading of organizational development and that the availability of a multitude of such problem-solving techniques attests to the richness and variety of the concept. The unschooled manager might think that the mere application of the right method to solve the problem in a particular area will do the trick. The more sophisticated management man is assured that all of this comes under the heading of organizational development—eclectic though it may be.

No one can foretell what sweeping fad will next appear upon the scene and profoundly affect the state of the management art, but some things can be predicted. A concept will be presented in broad and complex terms. Earnest and forward-looking managers will jet to various watering places where they will be inducted into the new thinking. The terms and notions in the innovative idea will become bastardized in common use. Some managers will see results and conclude that it works, others will deem it a flop. Ultimately it will all die out, to be replaced by yet another new concept.

Meanwhile executives will be doing their regular jobs under increasingly difficult conditions, perhaps wistfully realizing that a good many things they do are not what Peter Drucker calls true management. Nevertheless, they must do their jobs and try to remain healthy and sane in the course of their efforts.

The Concept of the Disposable Manager/3

The executive suites of thousands of corporations in the United States are filled by men who have become professional eunuchs. The drive and potency they once possessed have been spent. The native abilities and skills that gave them impetus as they began the climb to high corporate status have now vanished. They spend their days doing things that often seem meaningless.

This is true at the levels near the top. Just below, in the jam-packed ranks of middle management, thousands of men are on their way to becoming eunuchs. Oh, they still know how to do specific things and accomplish concrete goals and solve definite problems, but more and more they are cut off from actual contact with these realities. They are forced into a milieu of charts, figures and printouts, and told that the executive task does not consist in doing things yourself, but rather in antiseptic planning and decision-making.

This does not happen by accident, or through stupidity or mass hypnosis. A grand design diverts competent and even gifted people from what they do best and enjoy most. And this process of corporate emasculation takes place as an integral part of the management philosophy that has dominated American business for decades. This philosophy is embodied in the simple concept of the interchangeable manager and may be put this way: A manager is a manager is a manager—whether his company sells toys or turbines, insurance or insulation, computers or crackerjacks. The idea of management as a pure art, divorced from the nagging details of the particular business in which it is practiced, has been preached widely and effectively by the American Management Association.

Managerial interchangeability does not necessarily mean that the offices of president and board chairman are usually filled with men who have come to the posts from widely varying industries. Corporate wedlock, as we will be discussing, still seems to be a surer way to the top than job-hopping. Nevertheless, the principle operates even on a man who spends his entire career in a single company, because the higher he rises, the less his experience and feel for the particular work are valued. Current management thinking, as we pointed out earlier, claims that a gifted manager moving into a top policy job need know only four things:

> The company's legal position
> Its philosophy
> Its long-range goals
> Its budget

Nothing about what the company makes and sells! If the aspiring manager does know about these things, he is encouraged to forget about them, or at least to soft-pedal them. He is not to get his hands dirty by becoming involved in the nitty-gritty. He is to become a hothouse creature, breathing only the purified air of the boardroom in which only the big picture is ever contemplated.

From an overall strategic point of view, this emphasis on the pure art of management and the interchangeability of its practitioners seems to make sense. For one thing, the needs of organizations change. "Horses for courses" is what they say at the track, and companies also require different kinds of management leadership at different stages of their development. Typically, a new enterprise may be started by an inventive man who has come up with a new idea that fills a definite and current need. His business booms. He is the dynamo, his imagination and drive keep it going—but only up to a certain point.

That point has been determined within rough limits. In a fascinating study of *The Small Business Executive,* three men (Erich T. Prien of Memphis State University, Joel T. Campbell of the Educational Testing Service, Princeton, and Jay L. Otis of Case Western Reserve University) took a hard look at the business-building entrepreneur. They found that the driving entrepreneur was able to get the enterprise going through a certain combination of qualities, but that those same qualities became disadvantages at the point when the small, thriving business might turn into a large business. As they put it, "it was obvious . . . that a particular pattern of personality and leadership was necessary to start a small business and to develop it to the point where it had some stability [but] these behaviors and drives . . . were such that they would interfere with the growth of the business beyond the point where it could be controlled by one individual." The researchers observed that the typical enterpreneur was able to build the business up to, say, 200 employees, but "it is at this point that the organization will, and in a number of cases did, become stagnant." Others who have studied this phenomenon place the entrepreneurial level of achievement at around $7 million.

Obviously, different leadership is required beyond a certain point, which is why we so often see a pattern like this develop at the top of growing companies over a period of time: entrepreneur followed by administrator, then marketer, then financial wizard, then husbander of resources. This explains why the founder of a business is so often let out to pasture, usually, but not always, with plenty of green money on which to graze—Colonel Sanders of fried-chicken fame, Mr. Collins of Collins Radio, etc. Sometimes, as in the acquisition of Collins Radio by North American Rockwell, the supposedly essential new leadership comes in the form of a merger or absorption by an established organization.

Of course when something like this happens, the men at the top don't know much about the details of the business. But who cares? They are management experts, they don't have to know the business. In this book we are principally concerned with what this prevailing management philosophy does to men, not to businesses. But it is worth noting that more than a few companies find the lack of men at the top with a real feel for the organization and its problems can hurt. We recall a case in which the executive vice president of a consumer products company, who had long been regarded as a real management comer, was made head of a very large building concern. He had all the credentials and all the tools that today's management thinkers consider necessary, but at the time he took over, a veteran in the construction field remarked, "This guy won't make it." When asked why not, he said, "Because he has no feel for the business. He hasn't got that gut reaction of warning that you need in construction, with the kind of wheeling and dealing that catches you short on your cash-flow position. He won't grasp this until it's too late." And sure enough, a few months and millions of lost dollars later, the board replaced the president.

Even an organization like General Motors, which traditionally promotes upward from the assembly line, can get trapped by overreliance on the concept of interchangeability in management. The scene of the calamity was the GM Vega plant in Lordstown, Ohio, early in 1972.

Smarting in pride and pocketbook from the long-term inroads of Volkswagen, the more recent incursions of Toyota, and the mounting competition from small imports of all types, General Motors decided to put its chips on the Vega. Compact, sporty-looking, low in price, the Vega is built at the GM plant in Lordstown, just south of Warren and within about fifty miles of Cleveland, Akron and Youngstown. From management's point of view this is an area with a rich reservoir of skilled labor. Furthermore, that talent should theoretically be eager to get and hold jobs, since a slump in steel, rubber and manufacturing recently led to a local unemployment percentage well above the national average.

The top brass at GM knew that if the Vega were to be truly competitive, the critical elements in its production were efficiency and cost control. So a new management team was brought in to meet the challenge. The building of the Vega was turned over to the General Motors assembly division, a management group that has won a considerable reputation for hard-nosed cost-cutting and for getting the job done. Lordstown, it was reasoned, had not been turning out Vegas at peak efficiency. The new team would change that picture around.

Moving in swiftly, the new managers reorganized the Lordstown operation. For the most part this involved restructuring functions to make the assembly line faster and more efficient. True, in the process, some jobs and workers became redundant and were thus phased out (euphemisms come heavily into play when one addresses such a ticklish subject; in another area a brilliant practical semanticist coined the term *harvesting seals*). Jobs were eliminated on a chart in an office. When the chart was acted on, people were fired. However, the overhaul of the Lordstown operation involved a good deal more reorganization than elimination of jobs.

The target was to bring the assembly line up to somewhere near its full potential, 100 Vegas per hour. This was the key to remaining cost-effective in the current competitive market. As plans progressed toward fruition, everything looked good. The flow charts checked out, the sophisticated plant equipment measured up, and there was no reason to doubt the ability of the work force to produce. These were people who were getting more than $4.50 an hour plus added benefits coming to an extra $2.50 per hour.

The Vega is a simple car, simple to operate, simple to service, simple to build. It's designed that way. It has

43% fewer parts than a full-sized car, making assembly easy and quick.

The new managers stressed making various assembly-line functions simpler so they could be handled more quickly. But simplification was not the only principle put to use. There was also some additional detail work. A man who tightened four bolts on a clutch housing, say, would now also snap a spring into place. Probably there seemed every reason why he would be glad to do this. Plenty of people in the area were out of work, he was lucky to have a job. Certainly his work was not hard. Good design had practically eliminated heavy lifting and hard physical labor in the plant. He had easy access to the part of the car on which he was working, there was no crawling in and out as was the case in older, less efficient plants. Even the landscaping of the plant has been designed so that the worker had only a short walk from the parking lot to his job station.

The hard-nosed management plan swung into action—and the results were disastrous. GM estimated that it lost production of about 12,000 Vegas and 4,000 Chevrolet trucks in not much more than a month. There were times when it seemed that every available foot of paved space around the plant was filled with new Vegas, waiting to go back into the plant for repair before they could be shipped to dealers. Shipments, and concomitantly sales, dropped off drastically.

What was happening? For one thing it was simply a matter of people not doing their jobs. Astounded managers watched an engine block on the line moving past 40 men without one of them doing the job he was supposed to do. Obviously, if even one man skips his operation on one part, his omission has an effect. It may cause an immediate pile-up on the line because the job done by the man at the next work station may depend upon that performed by his neighbor. Or perhaps the omission goes through and is not caught until a later stage or the final inspection. Or perhaps the car is shipped out, only to cause later headaches for the owner, the dealer and the company.

But the problem goes beyond omission of functions. Management claims, and union admits, that there is sabotage. Vegas approach the end of the line with broken-off side mirrors, slashed upholstery, bent turn-signal levers and ignition keys, fractured windshields—even clogged carburetors. Instead of building cars, assembly-line workers are junking them. Meanwhile the battle against the small imported automobile is being lost even before the Vegas get off the assembly line.

Why is it happening? It's "the fastest line in the world" says the president of the UAW local. As he tells the workers' side of the story, it seems simple enough: Fewer people doing more work. Jobs have been eliminated and the remaining jobs have been not only speeded up, but added to. "You've got 40 seconds to work with. You add one more thing and it can kill you. The guy can't get the stuff on time and the car goes by. The company then blames us for sabotage and shoddy work."

Management insists that it is not as simple as all that. For one thing, according to the plant manager, "We're getting problems in areas where we haven't changed a thing." Management stresses the workers' lack of pride in the product. It deplores the don't-give-a-damn tendency to let shoddy work continue down the line.

Is it just the worker? There is testimony and some evidence that the problem spreads up to the supervisory level. Typically, a quality-control inspector reports that he told his foreman about a gap between the instrument panel and the body of the car. According to the worker, the foreman's response was, "To hell with it! Ship it to the dealer." The anonymous inspector attests that he refused to sign the inspection approval sheet, so the foreman signed it himself. Management admits that it is not anywhere near knowing the answers. Obviously there is a need to find some answers fast. In one month the plant received more than 6,000 complaints from Vega dealers; this exceeded the combined total of dealer complaints coming into all other GM factories.

In line with a current business enthusiasm, management has instituted sensitivity sessions in which the brass sits down with the workers and talks things over. This is described as an effort to find out what the workers' complaints are, but the complaints, and the attitudes behind them, seem plain enough. One man: "I actually saw a woman in the plant running along the line to keep up with the work. I'm not going to run for anybody. There ain't anyone in that plant that is going to tell me to run." It probably would not take any elaborate sensitivity sessions to elicit similar remarks from a great many people in the factory.

However, the overall management strategy has been one of toughness. Supervisors are told to discipline workers by sending them home without pay. Of course there is a further built-in financial penalty: when laxness or sabotage slows down or stops the line, workers are sent home early and are not paid for the lost time. Further, there are threats of punishment and firing.

Management seeks any ray of hope it can find. In June 1972, GM Chairman Richard Gerstenberg boasts that the company is recalling fewer cars than in the past. *Time* (July 17, 1972) quotes Mr. Gerstenberg, "We build them better—much better." The next day Chevrolet dealers were told to get ready for the biggest recall yet of the Vega, some 500,000 cars. The rear axles are defective. *Time* says, "The latest error was caused by workers on the speedy production line. Just how, nobody really knows." Chevy's manufacturing manager declares, "We made a terrible mistake, and the worst part of it is we just don't know how it could have happened."

A confused and dismal picture. A cloudy future for the Vega. Difficult and disheartening days for the management team. Could it have been done another and better way? Some industrial engineers and psychologists feel that Vega management went down the wrong road. For some time, influential behavioral scientists have been voicing increasing skepticism about the true efficacy of fragmented and highly specialized work arrangements. Early in our century Henry Ford gave us two revolutionary concepts, the assembly line and the $5.00 day. But we may now be coming to the point where, however much you pay a worker, he will so despise a repetitive assembly-line job that he will not be productive in doing it.

Within the past couple of years, industrial researchers have achieved some interesting results by taking an opposite tack. They have given the worker more, rather than less, of the job to do; they have moved back toward a bench-assembly operation and away from the production-line idea which has been in common use and acceptance for so many years. For example, in a factory assembling portable radios, the workers had previously been stationed along a line, each performing one function, each adding one tiny instrument to the finished radio. In an experiment, following some modest training, the same workers were assigned to put together large components of each radio. Some might even have been said to be building the whole radio. The result? Morale went up. Employee satisfaction grew. Turnover and absenteeism went down. These things, some of the researchers had predicted. What many had not predicted, however, was that productivity would climb.

Now a lot of authorities are looking askance at the assembly line. Recent studies into the concept of job enrichment suggest better ways to allocate work. The pioneering studies of Herzberg, among others, have cast doubt on the proposition that you can give a man the most boring job imaginable and be sure that he will continue to do it reasonably well, just so long as you pay him enough. If this were ever a valid idea, it does not seem to be valid anymore.

The truth is that on a national scale employee indifference—and in many cases active sabotage—has taken a sharp upswing. The broken half of a popsicle stick jams open the safety control on a punch press; a washing machine is delivered with three loose nuts dropped into the agitator space; a secretary, annoyed at having to work late, tears up $15,000 worth of accounts receivable and flushes them down the toilet. Unfortunately, rank-and-file employees are not often found in a sunny frame of mind these days, but then who is?

Some pundits are saying that we are all unhappy, all tired, all sick, all alienated, all disillusioned and turned off from the dream of a young country and a young people.

However this may be, the manager cannot cite this to his boss or to the stockholders to explain his failure to run an effective and profitable operation. No wonder the executive is uncertain and insecure. He is in deep trouble. The approved methods and concepts, which seemed to work so well only last year, just don't work today. They don't work because people don't seem to act and respond the way they used to. What is the manager brought up in the tradition of managership going to do?

Many are going to lose their jobs and not find others. We are already seeing it. Some will crack under the strain: neurosis, divorce, alcohol. Many will go on trying to do their jobs as long as there is a job to go to. We can no longer ignore the fact that professional management has not proven itself to be the modern philosopher's stone. Meanwhile management looks for answers.

Where might General Motors have looked for answers in the Vega situation? We cannot say precisely, but we can say this. An assembly-line job looks different from the plant catwalk than it does from the dust and bedlam of the factory floor. (How many executives involved in running large assembly operations have ever read *On the Line* by Harvey Swados?) Jobs and job functions can be restructured on charts, but people cannot be restructured into those jobs.

The point is that an interchangeable manager who moves from one location to another within a large corporation is not likely to have an instinctive grasp of the particular problems and circumstances in the new area. How can he be expected to? Of course, in the case of the man who moves from one industry to another— say, from tobacco to construction—it would be absurd to expect him to develop anything like a gut feeling for his new business.

Well, so what? The AMA says that you don't really need to know the business, that a thorough command of the tools of management will make you a success. It's not true anymore. A manager can't be recycled like a bottle. The situation has changed. The tools of management are no longer enough. As we move ahead in the '70s, it's going to take more than professional management to run a business, it is going to take natural management. He can operate on the basis of instinct as well as technique. In some ways natural management is a lot easier; however, for the man who is steeped in rules, it may be very difficult to understand.

What the Corporate Eunuch Has Going for Him –and Against Him/4

The daily life of a corporate eunuch need not by any means be a dismal one. True, if a management man is constantly thinking about the emptiness of his executive activities, he will be unhappy. But he doesn't have to think about such an unpleasant topic. Most of the people he meets face more or less the same situation, and fish swimming in the sea do not complain to each other that they are wet.

Millions of man-hours are consumed every day as people at various levels of management discuss, ponder and execute the minutiae of managership. It keeps them busy, and they are paid well for it. If this were all—if management life were a completely closed system— then those within it could be said to have achieved a permanent state of happiness.

But the trouble is that no system is ever completely closed. Eden was the ideal closed system, but the serpent opened it up. The fish's problem is not that he is wet, but that the water in which he lives is losing its oxygen, or that another fish will inevitably eat him. The most hermetically sealed system eventually breaches. It can happen slowly and insidiously, or swiftly and disastrously.

So long as the system retains a reasonable amount of its tightness, everything is fine for the management man. His working life seems full of movement and challenge. For the most part there is no real movement or real challenge, but the facsimile can be as much fun as the actuality. He is not doing anything really important, but what he does is regarded as important within the system. He is busy, often exhaustingly so, and to be pressured to the breaking point is a badge of honor within the system. Complaints about the unbearable loneliness and tension of management responsibility are rarely unalloyed complaints. They are almost always spoken or written about with a certain measure of pride and self-satisfaction.

Life within the system is seductive. Real power and genuine effectiveness are not such important commodities when the privileges of power are present. The trappings of potency and status are available on all sides for even the most functionally castrated executive.

We are familiar with the obvious trappings: the large corner offices, the thick carpets on the floor, the impressive originals on the walls, the keys to the executive washroom (which do exist), the rides in the company jet. And the secretaries. Not every manager, by any means, is galvanized by the sight of a shapely knee, but the attractiveness and "with-it-ness" of the secretary is a symbol of achievement as well as a congenial topic for badinage in the men's room and around the lunch-table. Whatever other kind of a piece she may be, the management man likes his secretary to be a good conversation piece. And of course this outlook, plus other social factors of which we are becoming increasingly aware, is making the really capable and effective secretary a rarity. While there has never been a study on the subject, we would venture a guess that some currently horrible examples of executive ineptitude can be attributed fairly directly to current lack of a reliable corps of skillful secretaries to take care of the business.

Perhaps the most distinctive boon—and ultimate bane—conferred upon the manager is the privilege of isolation from reality. The sales manager or vice president of marketing no longer has to cool his heels for an hour waiting for a half-drunk prospect to come back from lunch, or endure the agony of sitting still while a buyer coolly explains, "We have no complaint about the service you've given us over the years, but we feel that we've found a supplier who is more in tune with the needs of today." (Translation: I'm in hock up to my eyebrows on the races, and this salesman is willing to send it along under the table.) The production executive is remote from the dust and din of the factory floor, the bitter acid fumes of the plating vats, the stupefying foul-ups on the loading dock, and the cynical undermining of the shop stewards. The comptroller, immersed in the cool green depths of fiscal philosophy, does not have to trek all over the operation in search of data to complete sloppily filled-out job tickets, or cope with the vituperative foreman who wants to know why his machine operators did not get their overtime for last week.

The management man is remote from these things. If he has gone to the right school, secured the proper degree, and come up through the appropriate channels, he has never even been exposed to them. For the management man, much of reality is simulated and predigested, coming to him in a form that will never dirty his hands or sully his mind. The venal customer, the gold-bricking worker, the lazy clerk, their sweaty and malevolent existence reaches him only in the palest of reflections, in reports or printouts. Even the man whose success or failure depends upon his ability to understand what customers want, even this man need no longer go out and talk to the customers. The computer will fabricate a model of the marketplace for him.

And so the manager's well-rewarded day passes in relative isolation from reality. He reads the correspondence that his secretary has neatly arrayed on his desk and then he dictates politic and muted answers. He meets with colleagues, superiors, or subordinates, and even if the air all around is fetid with the odor of impending disaster, the atmosphere of the conference room is pleasant and antiseptic. All present are brothers in the system. They may be out for each other's blood, but blood is never actually spilled. And very seldom is sweat actually sweated.

A man can grow comfortably accustomed to this kind of life. When he feels the need for change, he can travel to a branch, an overseas operation, a convention. And always, even on the plane, he is within the system. Aloft, the secretary walks up and down the aisle to bring him coffee instead of coming in and placing it on his desk. If the manager attends a convention, he can be sure that he is still within the system. He is accorded deference, first-class treatment and even some measure of titillation.

All of this may tire him out. He may agonize over decisions and wrestle with plans and budgets, but there is still the carpet on the floor, the coffee-bringing secretary, and the soothing figures on the paycheck. His wife may be unhappy and his children disgusted; still, he is delivering the goods.

It can be a very nice way to live, or it would be a nice way to live if only there were some means of keeping the system closed. But there isn't. For every manager, the system opens up in one way or another, or in a combination of ways. For one thing, there is input to the system as younger men push their way upward. The balance must be maintained, and so the system ejects as well as accepts. The opening of the system may come through the process of aging; the manager over forty finds himself naked. Corporate competition may effect a breach in the walls of the system; the company may diminish under pressure, or even disappear. And then there is the most insidious of ruptures in the system, the opening from within. The management man asks himself what he is doing here. Is this really a life? The answer is troublesomely unclear—and the abyss begins to yawn.

The management man discovers, for example, that the same gentlemanly closing of ranks that tends to insulate the manager from difficulty and embarrassment will now close—against him. The boss who was previously receptive to his ideas, his problems, and even his random thoughts, now is often too busy to see him. "I'm up to my ears now, Jim, but let's grab some lunch early next week and we'll go over the whole thing." Colleagues continue to be affable, but where once they were candid in discussing their thoughts, they now turn the conversation into innocuous and meaningless channels. Even subordinates are different. One sales executive in the throes of the agonizing realization that his job was in real jeopardy said to us, "It dawned on me when I came back from a trip and sat down with my assistant, Tom Reed. Tom is a bright, eager boy and had always been as loyal as they come. I had seen him through a lot of his growing pains with the organization.

"Now I said to Tom that the first thing we ought to take up was the problem of getting the credit department to revise its ground rules on the acceptance of a certain new class of account. Tom, to give him credit, looked a little sheepish, and hemmed and hawed some. I thought he was going to tell me that it had slipped his mind and that he had not pulled together the stuff I had asked him to have ready. On the contrary. He said to me, 'Well, I think we have that straightened out.' Tom had gotten a bright idea on his own . . . and on his own he had gone to the president and to the financial VP. The new plan was already agreed to; it was a fait accompli. Tom said, 'I would have called you, but I knew you were busy . . . and I was pretty sure you would be in complete agreement with what I proposed.' I complimented him on his initiative and we got through the rest of the conference. But I was thinking to myself, That SOB smells something—and he's after my job! Brother, that was a shock. And it was only the first of many."

The manager who is in trouble with the system feels frustrated at every turn. It's almost impossible to go into his boss and say, "Let's have this out once and for all." That's risky—it might be precipitating a confrontation that might never come to pass otherwise—and besides, it just is not done.

So he waits and goes through the motions. It's important to keep up appearances, so he makes a real effort. On the surface he is still the same self-confident, high-riding knight of the corporate feudal system that he has always been, but inside, things are eroding away. Rarely does he go home and tell his wife. He hasn't kept her in touch with what he has been doing for years, and he certainly isn't going to walk in and say, "Honey, I'm in trouble."

He thinks about another job. Maybe he even makes some active effort toward testing the market for another job. But such moves made under pressure can backfire. When the job comes looking for the man through the medium, let's say, of an executive search firm, that's one thing. People in that profession know how to maintain confidences. But through inexperience the harried manager's efforts are apt to be indiscreet. Somebody from another company happens to be talking to one of his colleagues on the golf course and remarks, "Say, I saw so-and-so from your place the other day. He was in to see our people about something." And pretty soon the news is out. The manager's superiors now feel quite justified in actively seeking a replacement, if they have not done so already.

The management man who is in this situation has very little chance of turning things around through his own redoubled efforts to show that he is really irreplaceable. First of all, he is probably eminently replaceable. There is no particular thing he does for the company that will be done much worse if he is not around to do it. His functions are indirect, often intangible, and above all, difficult to evaluate. Bottom-line results can't be traced back to what an individual executive did. So it is not hard for top management to contemplate a change with the serene assurance that the organization will certainly be no worse off. Anyway, a little fresh blood might help.

Furthermore, the manager who has fallen out of step with the system is not going to increase his effectiveness, no matter how late he stays, how much he worries or how hard he works. More than likely, his effectiveness is apt to be severely diminished. His mind is not clear, his contacts are faulty. It is not a matter of losing real power, he has never really had any. But loss of the semblance of potency can be just as painful.

On any given day the commuter arteries will contain a significant proportion of management men who are in trouble, who are trying to stem growing leaks in the system's dikes. These men cannot be distinguished from their more secure fellows. Every one of them looks alike, confident, on-top-of-it, crisp, but the anguish quotient on, say, the 7:44 out of Westport is pretty high.

This is when it gets tough. Up to this point the manager has had it pretty good.

The question is, was it worthwhile?

The Hole in
the Busy Day/5

We'll call him Charlie Robinson, a vice president for a consumer-goods firm. He heads up the brand group and makes $47,000 a year. That's salary. In addition there are the bonuses, and of course there is the stock. Robinson has 500 shares. It's not paid for, but the company arranges for the loan.

Robinson is 44 years old. He has a house and an acre of land assessed at $80,000. A nice place, clean air, good schools and yet only 40 minutes from the office.

It's 7:15. Robinson has been home for half an hour. He thinks he'll have another drink—his third—before dinner. Then what? A movie? No, too tired. Besides, brought some work home from the office. Get to it after dinner, then watch some TV, then to bed early. A tough day tomorrow.

Mrs. Robinson wants to know when they are going to be able to take that long weekend and go upstate to see her mother and father. Robinson: "How the hell do I know? I work my head off all day and I have a briefcase full of stuff. I'm not sure when we can get away. Things are rough at the office right now." Mrs. Robinson doesn't bring up the subject again. Debbie, who is in high school, goes up to her room. It's best to stay away from Daddy. He's had a tough day.

After dinner Robinson goes into the study. He opens the attaché case and leafs through the material. There is one long report he's been meaning to get to for a week now. A couple of shorter reports. The monthly project list from the agency. Some memos, one from the president, asking for comments on the findings resulting from the recent study of costs conducted by Booz, Allen, Hamilton. That memo is going to require some thought before it is answered.

Robinson places the president's memo before him, squaring its corners away nicely with the corners of the desk. Next to it he places a full lined yellow pad. The pencils from the pencil holder, which had been made by Debbie in ceramics class and given to her father some years ago for his birthday, are not sharp enough. Robinson inserts three pencils in turn into the electric pencil sharpener, cocks an ear to its whirring, watches the flickering light that indicates the pencils are sharpened. He tests the points on his thumb. They are nice and keen.

Robinson is restless. He can't seem to get down to it. He gets up from the desk, takes a couple of strides and then three strides back the other way, bringing him to the wall. His tie is already loosened, he takes it off and throws it on the black, vinyl-covered reclining chair. It's hard to concentrate. He has a slight headache, that third drink was probably not a good idea. Maybe it would be best to pack it in for the night, go in early and get a fresh start on this stuff in the morning. Robinson decides that's what he'll do. He picks up his tie, throws it on the desk, seats himself in the recliner, reaches forward and turns on the color TV. After a minute, he tunes in another channel. Not much there either. A competitor's commercial comes on and Robinson watches it with mild interest. It's the same old slice-of-life stuff. No lift or zip to it. Nevertheless, Robinson knows that the competitor is putting $2.5 million in billing against the campaign, and the item is selling.

He tries another channel. Never anything worth watching on television. He switches it off, leans back and thinks about some of the events of the day, but he is too tired to think in any coherent fashion. Robinson is empty, unfulfilled, unhappy. The notion comes, as it often does at such a point, of saying the hell with it all and going away some place to a new life. Maybe work up a little mail-order business; get together with some of the guys that feel the same way he does and start a consulting practice; open a pottery shop on the highway in Laguna Beach. But of course it's all ridiculous! This is no way for a grown man with responsibilities to be thinking. Might as well go to bed. Robinson replaces the material in his briefcase, closes it, snaps the latches in place and leaves the study, picking up his tie as he goes. He places his briefcase by the side door.

What kind of a day has it been that has led Robinson to this pass? Not one too different from any other. When he arrived at his office in the morning, his secretary had already laid out the new incoming correspondence in two neat piles on his desk, one urgent, one otherwise. He went through the urgent pile first: some distribution foul-ups, a problem with quality control, a hitch in the introduction of a new product, expressions of skepticism from certain high quarters about the results of interviews conducted in a city where another product was being test-marketed. Then, turning to the routine correspondence, Robinson found some things that should have been placed in the urgent pile: bad feedback from a large supermarket chain about certain new point-of-purchase material, a complaint from another brand group about excessive use of computer availability.

Robinson had talked to the secretary about this kind of thing several times, suggesting that maybe she should just put the stuff in one pile. Although she was by no means a star secretary, she had been hurt at the suggestion, and personnel insisted she was the best available. So he would just have to get along.

After answering whatever letters he could, he summoned three brand managers separately for brief interviews. Each was instructed to look into a particular new problem and come back with an answer within a reasonable time. That taken care of, Robinson had a few minutes to leaf through a report from the research department outlining a new method of sampling that they recommended. It was a little hard to follow and Robinson considered giving it to an assistant who could work up a summary of the report, but offhand, he could not think of anyone he would trust to do it. He decided he had better take another look at it himself when he had more time.

At 11, there had been the weekly meeting of division heads in the conference room. Nothing particularly new there. Money was still tight and certain expansion plans were described as still being in limbo. There was another reprise of the recurring top-management theme of high costs and what would have to be done to offset them. Although some of Robinson's fellow managers were finding this repetition wearing and ominous, he didn't know whether he agreed or not. It was certainly another damn thing to worry about.

Lunch with some colleagues and contemporaries in other divisions was part good fellowship, part business. Everyone at the table, particularly after a martini or a whisky sour, was competent, confident, articulate and absolutely self-assured. Robinson fitted right in and at one point he looked a little wonderingly at Murphy, a fellow vice president, who had already launched into one of his inimitable stories about high-level idiocy in the company. Robinson had heard it said, and had seen evidence, that Murphy's position might be a little shaky. There was every reason to think that Murphy was well aware of this, but at lunch it was the same old irrepressible "Murph." You couldn't change him.

After lunch, Robinson had a meeting with his brand managers. The previous week he had presented some thoughts and plans and was now trying hard to elicit useful reactions. He worked particularly hard to smoke out some opinions from Summerfield, the youngest and newest of his key managers. Summerfield, who was said to be a comer, had arrived four months ago from General Mills with impressive credentials. At the meeting Summerfield seemed to nod in all the right places and murmur the right things, but he didn't say very much. Directly challenged, Summerfield said, "Well, Charlie, there isn't any question that this is solidly underpinned with a lot of high-class planning and research. I don't see anything at all that I could quarrel with." After the meeting Robinson found himself wondering what Summerfield had really thought, and in the next moment he was asking himself why the hell he cared so much.

At 4, he greeted an advertising-agency account executive, who had just jetted in, to introduce the agency's new creative director and to go over some roughs for print ads. The creative director seemed absolutely sure of himself and well briefed on the account. The account executive had all the proper pieces of paper in order right up to the second. He was a very buttoned-up account executive, and the men from the agency gracefully turned down an invitation to cocktails and dinner, saying that they had things they wanted to go over. Robinson was just as glad. He valued the ability of an agency man to turn down such an invitation gracefully.

A busy day, but what did Robinson really do? The fact is, he really did not do anything. He *considered* the offerings of others, he in turn *communicated* his own thoughts and plans, he *criticized* the efforts of others, he *channeled* the work of subordinates, but what did he *create?* What did he *contribute?* There was a time when, to ask such questions, to express such thoughts, meant that one was immediately put down as a malcontent dedicated to impugning the businessman and rending the fabric of our society. But no longer. Psychologists, including some industrial psychologists, are expressing such thoughts and asking such questions. So are medical doctors and psychiatrists. So are serious students of our society. So are the women who meet the executive's train or meet him as he comes in the door. So is a whole generation of younger people. So are managers themselves.

In the final scene of *Death of a Salesman,* Willie Loman's friend gives the salesman his epitaph: "He

45

don't put a nut to a bolt, he don't tell you the law—he's just out there riding on a smile and a shoeshine." The man or woman caught in the intricacies of today's managership is not riding on a smile and a shoeshine. It takes training and experience to do what he or she does. The struggle is fierce and the manager must do his job superbly well. But what are the true standards by which he is measured? Against what criteria can he measure his own accomplishment? When he has finished a busy day, *what has he really done?*

The name of Frederick Herzberg is familiar to any manager who has seriously followed his craft. Herzberg is the generator of the theory that money by itself does not motivate a man to work. He states that there are two sets of conditions that affect the way in which we do our jobs. One set he calls hygiene factors, the most important of which are: company policy and administration, supervision, salary, interpersonal relations and working conditions. These cannot satisfy, they can merely keep a person from being dissatisfied.

Motivators, on the other hand, have the power to satisfy. These are the things that make people feel good about their work and thus work harder and better. Simple motivators are: the work itself, achievement, recognition, responsibility and advancement. Herzberg says, "The factors that lead to positive job attitudes do so because they satisfy the individual's need for self-actualization in his work. . . . Man tends to actualize himself in every area of his life and his job is one of the most important areas."

The words of Herzberg and his host of followers are considered to be aimed principally at the manager. After all, it is the manager's task to get things done through people. Thus it is up to the manager to help his people achieve self-actualization through their jobs. Only in this way can they like their work and do it well.

But who motivates the motivator? From what source does the manager get his own self-actualization? It's becoming more and more apparent that managers— Robinson is one of many—cannot derive self-actualization from a day spent criticizing, communicating, channeling. Such management activity, intricate and demanding though it may be, involves neither creation nor contribution. The manager does not put a nut to a bolt. At the end of the day or the week, or even the year, he cannot point to something and say, "I made this." Figures on a profit-and-loss statement do not provide self-actualization. A house in the country is a hygiene factor. The memos, the reports, the telephone calls, the printouts, these are paraphernalia of self-emasculation.

It does not have to be this way. The manager should put a nut to a bolt, should achieve self-actualization, a realization for himself in action and fact. He should contribute and create. In doing so, he will be a better manager for the demands of tomorrow. But there will have to be some changes made in the general and particular approach he takes to his job.

The Endless
Business
Conference/6

More than forty years ago Thornton Wilder wrote a play called *The Long Christmas Dinner*. The scene is a family dining room, and the action takes place without interruption over a period of a hundred years. Characters progress from youth to old age at this endless Christmas dinner, and when one dies he leaves the table. The empty chairs are then filled by members of the newer generation.

Similarly, modern management sometimes seems like one eternal business meeting. Of course the meetings vary in size and purpose, and the characters change, but for the executive who works in a meeting-oriented company, the effect can be as fantasy-like as *The Long Christmas Dinner*. Everything seems to center on the conference room. The intervals between sessions appear to be taken up principally with digesting the conclusions of the last meeting and preparing for the next one.

"Meeting-itis" is a stultifying and even stupefying

malady. Taken to extremes, as it so frequently is, it can lead to a sense of emptiness and frustration that makes a manager ask himself, "What in hell am I doing here?" Moreover, meetings too often are symptomatic of ineffective management. When you have the feeling that you are going to so many meetings that you can't get the job done, it is probably more than a feeling: you probably aren't managing as well as you could.

It may be that the meetings you attend are starting to get to you. You may feel that they take up too much time, that they are dull and unproductive, that the results actually do more harm than good. Your current attitude toward conferences may involve a portion of each of these viewpoints. If this is the case, then it's time to do something about it. By taking a few simple steps to alleviate your meeting problem, you can make yourself a more effective manager and feel better about your day's work.

Some meetings you call yourself, while you are summoned to others by an individual higher up on the organization chart. Let's start with the first general type, those conferences that are convened at your behest and at which you usually preside.

Practically everyone has heard one of the many jokes based on the opening, "You're probably wondering why I called this meeting." Well, let's wonder a little. Let's examine each of the meetings you call and ask, Is this conference *really* necessary?

Most meetings can be classified into one of three categories:

Regular sessions for the exchange of routine information

    Special meetings at which the manager conveys information and issues assignments

    Problem-solving conferences at which each participant is required to contribute to a specific undertaking or focus upon a particular departmental difficulty

    The regular departmental meeting is likely to have been going on for a long time. Sometimes it is misleading to say that the departmental supervisor calls such a meeting. Scheduling this particular meeting every week or month may have begun long before the manager took over the department. Very likely no one who attended the first such meeting is still with the organization. So it isn't exactly called, it is just there. New arrivals in the operation are told to attend the meeting as part of their orientation procedure.

    Just because a regularly scheduled meeting has been taking place for a long time does not cast doubt upon its value, but all long-established customs merit reexamination from time to time. The regularly scheduled conference takes a piece out of your day, and it eats up a part of the other participants' days as well. Since executive man-hours represent a precious commodity, the regular meeting is therefore worth a fresh appraising look.

    The first question is, why the meeting? Its nature may have changed considerably from what it used to be when it was first instituted, so *restate for yourself the purpose of the meeting.* Don't take anything for granted. Don't settle for some broad formulation like, "We need to get together once a week so that we can all keep up to date on what the others are doing."

Business has become very complex and specialized. Departments that formerly worked very closely together may no longer need to do so nearly as often. If the regular meeting is the kind at which the participants take turns talking about what they are currently doing and what their plans are, ask yourself about the relative usefulness of this information to a roomful of people. True, it may be generally interesting to learn that Bob Johnson plans to put in two more calculating machines. But now that the others know this, can they do their jobs any better? Of course you, as manager, have to be up to the minute on what your people are doing, and you may feel that this kind of meeting is the most convenient way of getting your information. But your own convenience is not everything, and you may be wasting the time of others in finding out what only you need to know.

Indeed, you may be doing more than consuming the time of subordinates who might be better involved in doing something else. You may be building headaches for yourself. Go back for a moment to Bob Johnson and his two additional calculators. Joe Kelly, also present at the meeting, hears Johnson's plans. Kelly is not really involved with Johnson, nor is he better off as a performer for being privy to Johnson's plans. But he may well go back to his desk and brood: "How come Bob gets to spend money on something like that, when I get turned down on something far more important because the budget is supposed to be so tight?"

Now you find yourself patiently trying to tell Kelly what you have already told him, along with giving him a wholly extraneous explanation of why Johnson's request was granted while his was not.

Chances are that Kelly goes away unhappy anyway. The people who report to you should be given all the information they need to do their jobs. But why maintain elaborate machinery to provide them with data that they don't need and that will lead to diffusion of effort, frustration and more waste of time?

Another question that should be asked about the routine information-exchange meeting is, Do the people at the meeting now get the information through other means? We are in what is being called the Information Revolution. People in business have quick and sometimes instantaneous access to all kinds of information. And this situation will now grow to almost unimaginable proportions as the new science of data communications progresses. Perry Crawford, senior systems planner for IBM, gives us an example when he tells us that soon every middle manager will have a computer console that is as easy to operate as a radio. With it he will be able to call away volumes of information at the flick of a finger. So, given the alternate means of access to data that are now being developed, the question about the relevance and value of a particular information meeting is given added dimension.

Finally, regularly scheduled meetings with the same people acquire a formalistic life of their own. The session becomes ritualized with tradition. The same questions crop up over and over again with no expectation that anything will ever be done about them.

Here is how one manager talks about such ritualistic meetings: "One of my hobbies is reading about Egyptian archeology. Some time back it struck me that the conference table in my shop is shaped just like a 'solar boat.' The solar boat was part of the funerary equipment that the old Egyptians used to put into the tomb with the mummy of the dead Pharaoh. The boat was outfitted and provisioned with jewels, ointments, wines, tablets, and so on. The idea was that the spirit of the departed king would cruise the skies forever in his solar boat. Sometimes they even buried a bunch of attendants to serve as crew.

"The shape of our conference table got me to thinking. Here we all were, three times a week, on our own solar boat. We're outfitted with fat yellow pads and pencils with nice sharp points on them and easel charts and water jugs. And three times a week at regular meetings we cruise the skies. But there's something dead about it. Not much happens that is really alive and has meaning for today. People say the same things they have been saying forever. Nothing is too trivial or cranky to be brought up at the meeting.

"One of my colleagues can be counted on, at least once a month, to launch into his tirade on how management must guide rank-and-file employees in taking better care of their feet. He's a good man, he does a good job. When he gets going on this, we look at each other and try not to smile. He gets mad if we do. But I have to ask myself why the hell we all go in regularly and sit around that table and tell each other things that don't amount to anything or that we already know."

A reexamination of regular meetings, focusing on the type, currency and relevance of the information that is exchanged, may lead you to certain conclusions. Maybe the meeting need not involve all those who now attend. Maybe it needs to be held less frequently. Or perhaps it can be eliminated altogether. Cutting out a useless regular conference can do wonders for productivity and morale—for others and for yourself.

If, on your way home some evening, you can say to yourself, Today I eliminated a time-wasting meeting, you have achieved a distinct accomplishment.

The regularly scheduled meeting usually has a multiple agenda with routine items of varying degrees of importance. The special, nonscheduled meeting is likely to center on one particular topic. Basically this kind of meeting is informational. You, as the manager, have something new to convey to your people: a new plan, some new company policy, new information that has a bearing on departmental operations, new directions that you must pass along to the staff as a whole.

When the agenda involves passing along information or instructions that have more or less the same importance to everybody, and when it is definitely beneficial that each participant know what all the others have been told, there is no question that a meeting is the most economical way of getting the job done. Yet the specially convened meeting can be frustrating and time-wasting.

One manager, who bears responsibility for marketing part of a line of small appliances, gives this view: "My boss, Larry Cassidy, knows his stuff. He does his homework and he gets things the first time. Larry is tough, that is to say, he is demanding of the best effort you have in you, but he is not the kind of guy to eat you out. He goes out of his way to hear the other side of the story and to listen to legitimate problems and ideas. But there's one thing he does that is beginning to drive me crazy.

"For instance, Larry calls a meeting. He gets up and tells us that he's got a couple of thoughts, but that they're pretty rough. He thinks that he may have something hot, if we can only get together and come up with a plan. He wants our help. So he throws the problem, along with his thoughts, open to the meeting and we wrestle with the job of coming up with a plan.

"Or at least we're supposed to think that we're trying to come up with a plan. But before long it begins to come to you, what Larry is doing is trying to get you to come up with *his* plan. He's got the thing all figured out already, but he doesn't want to be a dictator. He wants the rest of us to think that we're participating. But what we're participating in, whether all of us know it or not, is a guessing game to try to read Larry's mind. First one that suggests what the boss wanted to do in the beginning wins the prize.

"I'm not saying that Larry Cassidy is absolutely shut off from any of our thinking at all. He listens, and he will sometimes maybe modify a point or two in his original scheme. But really what he's doing is kidding us, asking us for our ideas when he just wants to hear his own ideas echoed back to him. And he'll keep the meeting going until this happens.

"Don't get me wrong. Larry is good, and the plan he comes in with is, I guess, always better than whatever we might come up with as a group. But then why doesn't he just tell us what he wants done? The way he does it now, it's a big waste of time. You feel childish doing it. And some of us feel we are being manipulated. And the hell of it is that he means well."

Today the manager is told over and over again that he must not just issue orders. The trend in management thinking has been to urge the broader participation of subordinates. So, in the example just given, the manager is following what he conceives to be the proper and current executive practice.

This can be carried to counterproductive extremes. The result is the kind of meeting that superficially, for the purpose of imparting information and seeking feedback, is actually a subliminal sales presentation by the man in charge. It is subliminal because he does not want anyone to realize that he is selling his own point of view. But more is involved than just the waste of time. If the manager has perceptive people working for him, they will see through this device. Its repetition will become wearing, increasingly insulting and ultimately obnoxious. This is the kind of conference that some men are reacting to when they say, "I just can't take it anymore."

The late Abraham H. Maslow was one of the pioneering industrial psychologists who formulated the hierarchy of needs upon which much of our current practice in employee motivation is based. But Maslow neither recommended nor condoned the kind of phony democracy exemplified by the conference in which the manager attempts to seduce his subordinates into thinking his way, without their realizing that this is what has happened.

Maslow felt strongly that discussion and participative management should not be indulged in as a charade by an executive who is truly and validly convinced that he has the answers. Not only is it wasteful, it is harmful. Subordinates catch on, and "they are less apt to work hard because the work is useless and senseless. Why should they sweat . . . to work toward the solution of a particular problem when they know all the time that the superior one can see the solution in three minutes? The tendency, therefore, is for all the others to become passive. By contrast, they feel that they are less capable than they actually are, and more stupid, too."

The manager also pays a price: he is "apt to get extremely restless in such a situation, and the strain upon his body is apt to be much greater because of the necessity for controlling himself and inhibiting his impulses. He may easily and quickly see the truth that all the others are struggling toward very slowly, and keeping his mouth shut can be physical torture."

Evaluate your own meeting pattern. If you are conducting a form of group seduction, in which you try indirectly to get subordinates to go along with your thinking, you are probably paying a toll in emotional wear and tear. Furthermore you may be generating increasing resentment among subordinates. And finally you are spending a lot of time at meetings trying to do something that is not worth doing—and really can't be done.

When you have a plan and you are convinced the best way to convey it to your staff is via a meeting, by all means convene the meeting. But use it to accomplish your primary purpose, without subterfuge. The meeting will be over faster and everyone will feel better about it.

Now we come to a third type of meeting, the real problem-solving session, as compared to the artificial kind we have just finished discussing. In this case the manager genuinely wishes to bring the full thinking of his department to bear on a situation.

The old saying, Two heads are better than one, is faithfully observed by many managers today. Group problem-solving has become an article of faith. The meeting at which a collection of individuals grapples with a difficulty is commonplace. Many executives consider it the single most frustrating element of their working lives. But of course it is necessary.

Or is it? Is group problem-solving all that we have come to think it is? Is the summoning of a meeting the best way to generate innovative and effective thought in a crucial situation? There is increasing evidence that it may not be. As just one example, psychologists at the University of Minnesota conducted an experiment with eighty managers within a large corporation. Each manager was presented with the identical problem. One group of managers was asked to come up with an individual solution. A second group was organized into four-man teams. These teams discussed the problem for half an hour, then each manager went to his desk, alone, to try to come up with the solution. A third group of managers was also broken into four-man teams. These teams stayed together. They discussed the problem and together they came up with a solution.

When the results were examined, it turned out that the managers who had coped with the problem individually came up with better solutions than those who had met briefly and then worked on the solutions by themselves. But both groups did far better than the group who had worked out team solutions from start to finish.

In analyzing the results, the researchers found that the managers who had worked on the problem individually had examined all the possible alternatives and come up with better and more imaginative solutions. Those who had worked as participants in a meeting had forged consensus solutions. They had gone right down the middle.

So there is some reason to doubt that a meeting at which the assembled people receive a problem and work on its solution always provides the best answer. If you have been conducting problem-solving conferences and are not absolutely satisfied with the results, it may be that you are getting the "average" rather than the best.

Since meetings are so time consuming, it might be revealing to take a different tack. Don't call the problem-solving meeting. Instead, give your staff members the facts as individuals and ask them to come up with answers working on their own. If one-by-one briefing is not practical, hold a meeting only for the purpose of laying out the problem and describing the circumstances, then turn people loose to solve it by themselves. At the very least it will be a novelty and people are usually stimulated by novelties. More to the point, you will be bringing individual creativity to bear. You will be more certain that all the alternatives will be examined and that the problem will not be met with the usual humdrum, watered-down consensus solution.

By examining all the meetings that you convene— their purpose, their membership, their content, their records of effectiveness—you may find that you can eliminate substantial hours of useless meeting time. If you are in doubt whether a regular meeting should be continued, cut it out for a few sessions. You don't have to explain that it's a test, just omit it. Then see how many people ask when the next meeting is going to take place and how many get along very well without it.

Not only does cutting out excess meetings save time, it may also encourage independent creative thinking. It can build resourcefulness. It can free you, along with your subordinates, for more productive and fulfilling efforts.

Naturally some meetings must be held, but your examination and evaluation of them may have led you to change their personnel and content, to conform better with current reality. Moreover, with a clear idea of what each session is supposed to accomplish, you can achieve your purpose and then adjourn. The meeting that lasts five minutes, and yet bears results, can be a novel and exhilarating experience for you and everybody else. There is no reason why it shouldn't be happening.

Should Managers
Be Married?/7

The president of a company is looking for a top production manager. He has called in a head hunter to find the right man. The president has given the executive searcher a picture of the organization, has commented on the immediate problems that the new incumbent will have to tackle, has offered a description of the job, and has discussed the characteristics that he thinks most important in a new manager.

Now the president sums up. "This is not a 9 to 5 job. The man we are looking for has to eat, live and breathe production in this organization. He is going to run into a lot of problems and frustrations—and he's got to have the drive and the guts to see it through. He'll have deadlines thrown at him and he must be able to change his priorities rapidly to get the job done. Of course he has to have a feel for people and be able to get along with them, and he must be able to manage his time so he is able to participate fully in the planning and policy-making discussions that the job requires. And above all, we're looking for a sane, stable, well-balanced, happily married guy."

This is a typical description. Search men hear something like it all the time, including that last line, "And above all, we're looking for a sane, stable, well-balanced, happily married guy."

Of course those final words are nonsense. Management is not looking for a sane, stable, well-balanced man at all. The description given is that of a single-minded neurotic. In the selection of executives for the most demanding and responsible positions, industry prizes neurosis, rewards it and fosters it. The well-balanced man is not what is being sought at all. If such a man somehow does get this job, he will have great difficulty in holding it.

Let's move forward in time a number of months. The top production job has been filled, and at the last minute the company has received a large order that involves regearing and retooling of the plant facility to make a special run. Much of this critical work will have to be done over a certain weekend in June, a weekend that the production manager and his family have long been looking forward to. They have planned a pleasant, relaxing, soul-renewing trip to the mountains. All the arrangements have been made. A truly well-balanced man would be likely to do everything he could in advance of the weekend: fully brief his subordinates and delegate to them that part of the job which has to be done. He would then go on the trip assuming that the health of his family life was as important as his job. Would this decision evidence stability and balance? Would it please management? No, of course not. The president would wonder if his production manager were as dedicated to the job as he ought to be.

A few years ago there was a great fuss over the practice of certain corporations to "hire" the wife as well as the man. These companies openly admitted that they evaluated the wives of job candidates as well as the candidates themselves. Would she be understanding and totally supportive of the man as he took on his demanding responsibilities? Would she be a social asset? Could she handle herself with the right combination of sparkle and submissiveness in social functions which brought her into contact with other company executives, board members and important outsiders? In all, would she be a satisfactory corporate wife?

There was a great outcry over all this. Cynically amused observers pointed out the resemblances to an Arabian slave market. Women of brains and spirit objected strenuously to being considered as so many talking dolls. Promising young men—targets for corporate recruiting efforts—flatly said that they did not mind in the least that they themselves were evaluated, but that their wives were to be left out of it. The controversy has died down. Some of the companies that experimented with this sort of gambit concluded that it was pointless and that it cost more than it paid out. Other companies continue to look the wife over, but they do it subtly and surreptitiously.

The existence of a wife and, depending on the age of a candidate, an appropriate number of children up to the limit of three, is still generally considered to be a plus factor when a man applies for an executive position. Nowadays one divorce is acceptable. Two or more may be looked at askance. (One of the most dedicated and effective executives we know has been married seven times, three times to the same woman.

63

But he owns the company and would be unlikely to hire an individual with a similar connubial track record.) After all, a wife is prima facie stability, and stability is still given as a desirable trait. However, what management really wants is not stability, but a monomaniacal involvement amounting to neurosis or, sometimes, psychosis.

We are considering two institutions, marriage and management. There has been a general tendency to think of these two institutions as basically harmonious. The support of a kind and understanding helpmate makes a manager more effective on the job. True, some executives permit the job to interfere with their home life, but this is just a matter of "poor planning" which can be rectified if the manager calls up the little woman more often, tells her more about his job and his problems, takes home less work in a briefcase, and so forth. It is also true that some individuals seem to permit their marriages to interfere with their job performance, but such persons are simply not cut out for high management posts and do not get ahead.

Perhaps it is time to face up to the proposition that a successful career in management today is the deadly enemy of a happy marriage. Of course this seems quite extreme. Whenever the point is made in this fashion, a host of protesting voices are raised. "Look at John Smith. He's eminently successful in his industry and has a fine wife and three happy children."

On the surface, such examples appear valid, but there is increasing evidence that beneath the surface something may be seriously wrong. Divorce statistics within the executive and professional ranks are alarming a lot of people. True, a division manager for General Foods may be able to afford a divorce, and a piece worker in a luggage factory cannot, but this economic argument falls short of settling the matter. Clergymen, psychologists, psychiatrists and marriage counselors have been pointing with increasing urgency to an apparent serious conflict between marriage and a management career. Women's Liberation can no longer be laughed off. It is bringing into sharp focus a broad-brush picture of unhappiness and desperation that underlies the surface pastel of affluence and contentment. The children of members of the management class—sensitive, perceptive and close to the scene—are rejecting with scorn and loathing the life style of their parents.

And now typical successful executives and their wives are beginning to be heard from. These are not exhibitionists or oddball malcontents. They are the people that have ridden the crest of the management-revolution wave in America.

Mortimer R. Feinberg and Walter Reichman, two industrial psychologists affiliated with Baruch College in New York City, conducted a study of the executive marriage with 300 executives and 200 wives of executives. The research took the form of detailed questionnaires and follow-up interviews. Superficially the combination of responses seems to describe an idyllic state. However, a closer look showed some startling contradictions, leading the researchers to characterize the executive marriage as "a very delicate mechanism requiring constant adjustment by both partners [and which] takes its toll in the form of suppression of feelings, guilt and anxiety." Suppression and guilt! Typically, the wife of a corporation president (39 years old, married 18 years) said, "My marriage is good in every way," then she added, "but I'm personally unhappy." Was this her husband's fault? No. "He is intelligent, loving, generous, understanding, loyal, dependable, ambitious, hard-working and has a sense of humor."

The feeling of guilt was not confined to executive wives. Husbands lamented that they could not spend more time and give more of themselves to their families. Said one, "My wife has been a mother and father to the children. It's been very hard on her but she's done a terrific job with them." Managers generally rationalize this guilt in various ways: "I'll make it up to them." . . . "I'm doing it for their sake." . . . "I couldn't do it without her." This last mechanism—making the wife a part of success in a management career—is particularly interesting since only 1% of the wives said that they were helpful in their husband's career.

The responses indicated a yawning gulf in communication between husbands and wives. While 70% of the managers claimed that no one else in the house felt the effects of their work problems, only 10% of the wives agreed with this. Sex was another problem. A marriage that is "good in every way" would certainly seem to infer good sexual relations, but fewer than 40% of the managers said that things were satisfactory in this area, and given the stigma that our culture attaches to inadequate sex, the figure is probably inflated.

Overall, the picture is one of intelligent and sensitive people who are fully aware of the conflict and compartmentalization existing between job and family. Out of a sense of duty, or "for the children," or just for the sake of appearances, there are strenuous efforts to paper over the gaps. Nevertheless, they remain, and they are painful. Wives feel unfulfilled, husbands feel guilty.

Naturally both parties seek to ameliorate the situation in various ways. On the executive's side this generally means taking his wife on trips, involving himself more in family activities on weekends, forcing himself to take an interest in what is going on at home. Many wives try to find something else to fulfill themselves. For a good number this takes the form of community work, and in recent years various volunteer organizations have found themselves fortunate indeed to be able to tap an increasingly rich reservoir of female talent. Other wives take jobs. Whether the occupation is voluntary or paid, the wife seems to be counterbalancing the involvement and struggles that her husband encounters on the office front.

Still other wives attempt to solve the problem by pouring more and more of themselves into the career of being a wife and mother. For some this may be enough, for others it simply does not work. Some wives—more than a very few—simply come apart. Drinking, drugs, sex. They implode as human beings.

The situation of many executive wives is eloquently summed up in a wife's letter printed by *Interpersonal*, a management bulletin: "Most women, too, want to make a go of marriage. What does *go* mean? Cars, for instance, run with varying degrees of efficiency. In how good repair are *both* partners willing to keep their marriage? The husband comes home so tired, he is mute. . . . Late in the evening my husband is too tired to tackle problems, and problems do arise. In the morning he wants a pleasant headstart on the day. Why not get a job? There are lots of reasons—child care, conflicting school schedules, low wages, and often as not, the most compelling reason, *the husband's non-negotiable objection*. . . . It's a two-way street. The husband must do

67

some 'creating' too. A man can give all to his job and save the emotional leavings for his home. But he'll get what he is asking for—success and an unhappy home."

Of course marital stress may be found at any point along the spectrum of our society and it is by no means confined to the managerial class. But there is increasing evidence that the executive job, which calls so completely for involvement of the whole man, creates its own special stresses upon the institution of marriage. Dr. Benjamin B. Wolman, a New York psychoanalyst who sees a great deal of executives, their wives and their children, states that the risks are much greater for the executive. "The manager carries such responsibility and his work demands so much of him that such things seem to happen to him more . . . and, of course, to his family." Managers are constantly subjected to the "temptation for them to become over-involved in their jobs—and they succumb to the temptation to the point that it affects their sex lives. They come home so tense that they show little sexual interest. First the normal affection goes out of the relationship. Sex becomes forced and scarce. The wife goes on a sex strike. The husband begins to run after other women. Sometimes I wonder if sexual problems are not part of the executive's life."

Let's talk about two people. You can find Bob Myer every morning in the facing seats at the end of the smoking car on the 8:10. Myer has played cards with the same commuting partners every working morning for four years. A tall, good-looking man with a healthy tan, a slight trace of gray at the temples, maybe in his middle thirties, maybe younger. He is always very well, but not snappily, dressed, looks alert, sharp and always self-confident. In other words, he very closely resembles his companions on the train.

You can hear Bob Myer as well as see him. He slams the cards down. He's always got a good story or a telling, but good-natured, put-down. He is a great kidder in a friendly man-to-man way.

Bob Myer is already successful and he's on his way to even greater success. Everybody knows that. Bob is very good at what he does. He is tough too. "How did I make out in Atlanta? Well, it was either that I would screw them or they would screw me. The big thing is to always be on the screwing end." He pays the price for working under pressure and he is not reluctant to tell you about it. "Sure, my doctor thinks I've got an ulcer coming on. A hole in the gut to match the one in my head. Well, man, I figure if you give ulcers, you got to get them. That's the membership fee."

Bob Myer has been sexually impotent for 15 months. Of this he does not boast.

After Mrs. Robert Myer gets the youngest of the kids onto the school bus and outlines the plan of the day for the cleaning woman, she reports to the civic council office. There's a lot to be done there. Five hundred copies of a mailing must be run off on the mimeograph machine. Then there is an interesting lunchtime meeting with a group trying to promote middle-income apartments in this high-level community. Mrs. Myer works very closely with the chairman of this group, a very dynamic and charming local lawyer, who has been divorced for about four months. The lawyer could use somebody with Mrs. Myer's skills in his office and he has told her so. During the meeting Mrs. Myer's mind wanders. She wonders what time Bob will be getting home. She thinks about a piece she read recently in *Life* about women who have dropped out. She again considers the job with the lawyer. She fantasizes about him in other— far less licit—contexts.

But none of this really seems to provide an answer.

In popular novels of the *Executive Suite* type, the core of the problem is presented as sex. The hero is a highly charged omnipotent person who is always coming into contact with glamorous and available women, notably his worldly-wise and nubile secretary. That pale little woman back home doesn't understand—she's a drag.

This picture is a highly misleading one. The conflict is not between more or less desirable sex objects. It is a conflict between career and home. When the demands of management become all-encompassing, as is frequently the case, the manager simply does not have enough left over in time or emotion for his family. The effects of this on his wife are beginning to become better known. We have discussed some of them here, but the effects upon the children need no elaboration. They turn on, they drop out, they go a different way. Look at the front page of your daily newspaper or turn on the television news.

Techniques like calling up the wife more frequently while on business trips simply do not offer an answer. The causes lie deeply rooted in the nature of the totally demanding management function. However, there are solutions, but they are not superficial ones. For the executive they involve an understanding and an accommodation, not merely with his wife and family, but with his profession and his future. There are things that a manager can do, but they may involve a very fundamental reordering of values and priorities. They may call for a sacrificing of objectives toward which a professional lifetime has been directed. They may demand utterly different insights into what even the most highly skilled and accomplished manager can expect to get out of the rest of his life.

Let us make a modest proposal. Maybe it would be best if young men who choose to enter the profession of management did not ever marry. There are parallels in history.

For 500 years the standing army of the Ottoman Empire consisted of the Janissaries, an elite military force. As children, they were taken from their parents. They were trained in all of the intricate arts of war. They were drilled in obedience and resourcefulness. Bravery and honor were instilled into them. Janissaries were never permitted to let their beards grow—or to marry. Marriage would have interfered with the single-minded dedication with which these professionals addressed themselves to their trade.

If our economy and our society depend upon an elite corps of professional managers, perhaps this corps should be considered the Janissaries of our day. At least a young man considering such a career might well think of himself as a modern-day Janissary—and consider very, very carefully whether marriage in any way conforms with his chosen life.

Of course there are thousands upon thousands who are already committed as the Janissaries of business. They feel guilt and compassion toward those they leave behind at home as they go off to the wars, they try to straddle and make the arrangement work, but the strain is enormous and ultimately, for many, impossible to bear.

71

The manager must make a basic decision. If he chooses to continue as a Janissary, there are certain truths—sometimes unpleasant truths—that must be faced. If he chooses to opt out of the elite, he must find a way to do it with dignity and a reasonable degree of security. For many managers, this is a decision that must be faced. It cannot be sluffed off.

I'll Go into Business for Myself/8

We have already met Charlie Robinson, the 44-year-old executive whose career seems to be turning sour on him. Of course we have not just met Robinson within the pages of this book. Most of us have known Charlie Robinsons at one time or other. You may know one now. Or you may be one now, for in a way, we are all Charlie Robinsons. There are few managers who have not passed through something like Robinson's frame of mind. If you have not yet experienced it, it may well happen.

Robinson is going through the motions. He does his day's work, but it has less and less meaning for him. He seems to read his reports, conduct his meetings and dictate his memos in a vacuum. As we have seen, there is little he can point to and say, "I did this all by myself." Pinned down, Robinson would be the first to admit that most of his accomplishments contribute little to the real world or to his self-image as a human being.

Robinson is going through a phenomenon familiar to many executives who have done well, but who have not made it to the top. They have reached the milestone of 40. The promotions and job offers that came swiftly and copiously in the early years are not so abundant anymore. They make good money, but the dollar doesn't go as far as it used to. No matter how much money they make, it never seems to be quite enough. The ascent up the corporate ladder has slowed, perhaps even stopped for some years. Nor is the view up the ladder as clear and unblocked as it once was, and the manager is uncomfortably aware of jostling on the rungs immediately below.

The industrial psychologist, Mortimer R. Feinberg, uses the term *middle-age megrims* to describe the situation so many executives find themselves in when they reach middle life. "The thrill is gone," says Dr. Feinberg. "The man's body and his mind are not quite what they were ten or fifteen years ago. He will not admit to himself that the natural processes of life are beginning to take their toll, so he blames it all on the job."

The manager who is afflicted with middle-age megrims begins to fantasize. "The way this place is run is unbelievable. You spend years telling people how to handle something, but nobody will listen to you." . . . "Nowadays they let these kids come in and take over the company. I'm looking forward to watching them fall on their faces." . . . "If I had taken that chance to go off on my own, I'd be sitting pretty now—but it's not too late. I'm at my peak."

The megrims affect the manager in a number of adverse ways. Mental channels are blocked. He cannot give to urgent problems the rational thought that they deserve. He becomes moody and perhaps more short-tempered. Others—his subordinates, his colleagues, his boss—notice the change and comment, "What's gotten into Robinson these days? I asked him to update me on something and he practically told me that it was none of my business. Charlie is a good man—always has been— but you begin to wonder if he can really cope with things anymore." The change in Charlie Robinson is not merely superficial. He really isn't coping with things up to his maximum capability.

This is not happening because Robinson is getting older. It is true that with the years we gradually lose some of the power of youth, but we usually compensate for the attrition by added experience and savvy. That is, we do if we have not worked ourselves into a what's-the-use corner, if we have not fallen prey to the middle-age megrims.

When many managers start to look around for a way to get out of the rat race, they tend not to look at the present. In their fantasizing they are not examining themselves and the surrounding circumstances as they really exist. They are not subjecting the pluses and minuses of the situation to cool managerial judgment.

Instead, they reach back into the past. Years ago Charlie Robinson may have seriously considered an opportunity to go off on his own and be his own boss. Most of us in management seem to have an innate memory or vision of entrepreneurship. H. L. Mencken set forth as part of the American Credo that "it is more admirable to be in business for yourself than to work for somebody else." Of course Mencken was being his usual sardonic self, but he was speaking the truth. When managership begins to pall on an executive, the solution may seem to be to go into business for himself. He may do it —and it may be a disaster.

We are not talking here about the man who moves to another managerial job, nor are we talking about the man who becomes a consultant, either by setting himself up independently or by joining a consulting firm. We are talking about the man who becomes his own boss by turning sharply from his previous path, starting over and going down a totally new road.

The idea is very much with us these days. In *Starting Over* (Macmillan, 1971) *New York Times* reporter Damon Stetson collected scores of case histories and anecdotes of people who have embarked on second careers. They have opened restaurants, established stores, taken over ski resorts, entered the mail-order business. The list is a long one, and obviously the focus of such a book is bound to be upon those who have been successful in their new ventures.

One might draw the superficial inference that anyone could do it, but Mr. Stetson is at pains to disabuse us of that notion. "There's no intention here to advocate a second career for everyone or even most people. . . . It is enough I think to point out that in today's world it may not be necessary to continue in a dull boring job or to go on indefinitely leading a pressurized, tension-ridden existence. There *are* opportunities for second careers, to gain greater self realization through your work, to start life anew if you are not happy and satisfied in your present way of life."

In his summation Mr. Stetson returns to the dangers. "There is no sure and certain avenue, however, to a second career. If there is one thing that the numerous examples in this book has demonstrated, it has to be that the route to a new occupation, to a different way of living and working is not clearly charted, that there is no precise pattern. . . . The risks are great and the hurdles high. Some live to regret their change."

The great burgeoning in recent years of the franchise concept reflects the breadth and depth of the wistful search for a new start in life. Franchise operations vary widely, but they all offer the prospect the chance to be his own boss. Yet franchising companies have been running into trouble. Some have had to go deep into the hole to buy back franchises. While training, plant, equipment, financing and support are usually adequate, and even though the individual who takes over the franchise may be intelligent and eager to succeed, he nevertheless fails because he is simply not cut out to succeed on his own.

There is good reason for this. A lot of managers feel that they carry an entrepreneur's baton in their knapsacks. It can be a consoling and inspiring thought, "but it ain't necessarily so." Why? Considering the many forces at work, it is extremely doubtful whether a man who has spent twenty years in the employ of others possesses the special qualities to make it on his own.

This never occurs to the frustrated and disheartened manager during those long afternoons or evenings when he dreams of escaping from the old rat race. Mr. Stetson tells us that "for each man who dares to embark on a second career, however, there are thousands who don't have the courage." All too often the decision to become an independent operator is based more on rashness and desperation than on courage. The big step is taken as a kind of hopeful suicide. The courage that impels a man to become his own boss must be accompanied by characteristics that will enable him to be a successful entrepreneur. When a man pulls out of the management pat-

tern, rat race though it may be, only to make a debacle
of his career, he may reach a point of real catastrophe in
his personal and professional life.

Listen to the experience of one who went through
it. Mr. B. G., a marketing executive, now 42, made the
big move to go off on his own. "I had had it up to here.
I was sitting at my desk reading pieces of paper and they
seemed like absolute gibberish. It was getting so that
every time my boss made even a mild comment, I took
it as a threat. The people who worked for me were
dummies—it was hard for me to hold myself back from
tearing their heads off. The only one in the whole place
who looked good to me was my 23-year-old secretary,
and she was looking too good. I was in real trouble.

"I was tired of getting pushed around by people
and by circumstances. Like everybody else, I had thought
from time to time that what I really needed was to be on
my own. To be my own boss, not a consultant, not a head
hunter. I wanted to get as far away from the executive
jungle as it was possible to get. Well, what were the
chances? What did I know?

"If there was one thing I did know, it was restaurants. Between here and Honolulu, I knew the best spots
in every town. Those years of taking big accounts to get
a hell of a good steak! I was going to make them pay off.
You see, I had a little money put away, not much but a
little, and there was the chance to open up this steak-
house franchise in my home town. It looked like it was
made for me.

"They put me through a training program and gave
me books to read and accounting forms and all the rest
of it, and I really plunged into it with enthusiasm. There
was no place there that you could get a really good steak

for a reasonable price. I was on friendly terms with a lot of the local businessmen, and I figured why wouldn't they want to eat in a place run by a man who knew something about what they did rather than just a straight restaurant man. Well, we opened up and they did come. I was serving a lot of steaks per week, well above what they told me was the break-even point.

"But I was in a hole and getting deeper every day. I had a big nut to pay off. It began to seem like landing a big national account was child's play compared to dealing with meat and vegetable and baked-goods suppliers. It was impossible to get help who were not morons. The one who did seem to have something on the ball stole me blind. It lasted six months. Now I'm an ex-restaurateur looking for a job. When I'm with my wife and kids, I find it hard to meet their eyes."

The executive who plans and directs the work of others in a modern corporation works under certain conditions. He comes to take these conditions for granted. They vary widely within the company and the industry, but there is one common thread: today's manager gets other people to do it, *he does not do it himself.* He directs, he delegates, he designates. This is the very opposite of entrepreneurship as Mr. B. G. and many others like him have found out to their discomfort.

Has the thought of going into business for yourself ever crossed your mind? If it has, or if it ever should, you should be prepared to answer a number of questions frankly. They are based upon intensive observation of those who made it on their own as against those who didn't.

Are you a pennypincher? Are you the kind of guy who makes sure the lights are out before you leave? Do you watch every stamp and paper clip? For many managers used to dealing with figures followed by at least three zeros, the answers to such questions must always be no. Everything in their background and training tells them to think big. They cannot think small. Yet, succeeding at your own business usually means thinking very small. Your margin is tiny. There is little or no leeway. If you are not the type who watches every penny, and, let's face it, many of us are not, then entrepreneurship may not be for you.

Are you handy? Do you enjoy doing detail work? Can you type a decent page? Can you repair simple machinery? In most organizations of any size, the manager just does not do these things. It is not his job. If he is seen fooling around with minutiae, he is looked upon as an oddball at least and probably as a man who is malingering because he can't face up to the big, broad challenges of high-level management.

Can you really evaluate the skill of rank-and-file workers? Can you really communicate with them? How do you detect whether someone is honest or dishonest? When you are in business for yourself, there is no personnel department to send up another applicant, there is no one to whom you can delegate the job of preliminary screening. Your success may depend heavily on the goodwill, ability and integrity of people with whom you have had little or no experience. Are you willing to put in long hours of hard, routine labor? Are you inured to solitary boredom, or have you taken for granted, as part of your professional way of life, the solace and stimulation afforded by having a variety of colleagues and contemporaries around you?

To what extent have you come to wear your status

like a seamless garment? True, you may be highly conscious of the bad things about the job, but what about the splendid lunches, the stimulating trips, the pretty secretary who dotes on you? What about the comfort and convenience of a tastefully decorated, well-designed air-conditioned office? It isn't shameful to like these things, they are enjoyable and can be conducive to effective work. They can also be habit-forming. Many executives who have escaped the corporate turmoil also find—a little late—that they have removed themselves, cold turkey, from a pleasant drug upon which they have long since become hooked.

Finally, how about your wife and family? As a manager you may have been able to compartmentalize your life, or you may have found that it became compartmentalized whether you wanted it that way or not. When you're on your own, for better or for worse, just as in the marriage vow, there is much more togetherness. This is not necessarily enjoyable. Indeed, it may not be the most salubrious climate for a healthy and enduring marriage.

These questions represent some of the points the would-be entrepreneur must struggle with. While it is true that many executives achieve inspiring successes in new careers, the qualities that tend to make a man an effective corporate manager are clearly not the qualities that make him a winner on his own.

A recent study supported by a grant from the Small Business Administration concluded that the successful entrepreneur is a one-man band. "He initiates, follows through, and brings to a point of closure both the minor and major, routine and critical day-to-day and long-term operations involving the organization."

This is hardly a description of a successful manager in today's typical corporation. But it may well describe what tomorrow's manager is going to have to be like. There are powerful movements abroad in the business world today, we are convinced, that will bring the profile of the successful corporate manager and the successful entrepreneur into far greater conformity than ever before. One might well say that we are coming, or returning, to the day of the entrepreneurial manager. Harking back to the 100-year history of the Ramsey company in Chapter 1, we may be completing a cycle. Old John Ramsey is coming back into style.

The Executive Emporium/9

We are all part of the management marketplace. Sometimes we are buyers, sometimes sellers. Often we buy and sell at the same time. A man sells himself to a new employer, and at the same time he buys a job that may be a dominant factor upon the rest of his life. An employer in effect buys a job candidate while simultaneously selling that candidate on the benefits of the job.

Often these transactions go on as if both parties were operating in the dark. The executive who is "looking" usually jumps at an offer without enough information to make a decision. The manager doing the hiring sees a likely candidate and grabs him. One or the other, often both, are sorry before too much time has elapsed.

This hurried and ill-advised decision on both sides— the offer of a job and the acceptance of it—accounts for much of the anxiety, distress and alienation that beset the manager today. When an executive is unhappy, his mind turns to change—job change. Manager Bob Smith may think, I've got to get out of this place before I get stuck in too deep a rut. I think I'll do some looking around.

In another company, Bill Jones, who sits in the president's chair, is deciding how he will resolve his own unhappiness with the way things are going: We've got too much dead weight in this organization. We've got to make some changes, but who can I rely on to do the job?

So Bill Jones begins to look for the right man, the self-starter who will pitch in, solve problems and get the job done—and in the process enable Jones to be more effective and happier in his operation. Where is Jones going to find this individual? He knows he needs help. To spot and screen the best possible candidates takes more time than Jones has at his disposal, even if he were an unerring judge of men. In these circumstances Jones may turn to an executive search agency.

The legitimate executive searcher is a highly skilled professional. His craft is fitting the right man to the job, but he is not a superman, nor is he a clairvoyant. Moreover, the final decision does not rest in his hands. He finds men based on his understanding of what the job entails, but he must seek candidates that he feels are acceptable to the employer. As we will see, these two considerations do not always go hand-in-hand.

Bob Smith has a good track record. He is a good candidate for the job that Jones has to offer, or so it seems on the surface. Ultimately Smith and Jones meet. They may be brought together by a search professional, but for our purposes the means is immaterial. From now on, the transaction rests in the hands of these two men.

Executive Smith is ushered into President Jones's office. They exchange greetings and shake hands. Jones says to himself, I like this man.

These superficial values that the applicant conveys

should not be very important in the job transaction. We might call them cosmetic values. They should not be very important, but they are, because the quick, favorable judgment that President Jones makes of applicant Smith may well overshadow everything that goes on between the two men.

Smith is over the first hurdle. Logically it should not be a hurdle at all, nor should the applicant, again logically, be very far advanced toward landing the job because he clears the hurdle. Nevertheless, this is often the way it goes and experienced search professionals know it. If Smith did in fact talk to an executive search professional, chances are the professional was able to predict the favorable chemistry.

On what basis does the president's initial good impression rest? Jones, if asked, would find it impossible to analyze. He might say, "I like his presence." Smith seems self-assured, he speaks calmly but unhesitatingly, and he appears to fit the part.

Appearance certainly helps to create a favorable first impression in a job interview. Tall is better than short, well built is better than thin or fat, a firm handshake is essential, the right suit makes a world of difference. Illogical as they are, these things mean much. Perhaps somewhere in creation there is another universe in which shorter men make the best initial impression and in which a flabby handshake and a shifty eye are prized as harbingers of excellence of character, but not here. These circumstances exist, and all those in the executive emporium must live with them.

This is not to say that every businessman gives an applicant, especially a managerial applicant, a job because he looks good, has an expensive haircut, and wears a tasteful tie. However, more often than not, the purely cosmetic traits of the jobseeker will greatly influence the interviewing process. Yet this can operate as a disadvantage, because an extremely favorable first impression may have an insidious and ultimately damaging effect on the perception of the employer. Jones is eagerly looking for the right man and as soon as he sees the personable Smith, an inner voice insists, This could be the guy. And so, instead of probing and evaluating as the interview goes on, Jones begins to sell Smith on the job. The president is not doing this consciously, nor is he doing it blatantly. It's only natural for a businessman to speak with pride of his own operation, but in his manner, his willingness to make allowances, his weighing of the pluses and minuses of the applicant, the employer is presenting himself, the company and the job in the most favorable light.

Of course he is looking the candidate over as well. Theoretically he is looking at the candidate to judge how well the man fits the organization and the assignment. All too often this does not really happen. Instead of looking for certain qualifications, experience, accomplishment and ability that apply directly to the task that will be assigned, the employer looks, rather, at certain generalized characteristics.

Not long ago Drs. Milton D. Hakel and Allen J. Schuh of Ohio State reported in *Personnel Psychology* (Spring, 1971) on an interesting research project concerning decision-making in the employment interview. They asked more than 5,800 employment interviewers a series of questions designed to isolate the attributes upon which they based their hiring decisions. After sifting and analyzing the responses, Drs. Hakel and Schuh found nine positive characteristics that appeared to be universal. The ideal applicant should be cooperative, be able to accept responsibility, be dependable, trustworthy, self-controlled, be able to get things done, be conscientious, stable and responsible.

As the researchers pointed out, these items seem to fall into two clusters. One cluster seems to relate to how well the applicant gets along with other people. In fact, several of the characteristics in this cluster seem to be saying the same thing in different words. The other cluster (dependable, trustworthy, etc.) "is much more difficult to interpret, but seems to represent the attributes of a good citizen. In fact, many of the statements qualify for inclusion in the Boy Scout Law."

At this point you might well ask, What kinds of jobs were these interviewers filling? Therein lies a revealing point. Employers placed about the same weight on these characteristics in evaluating people for each of the following job categories: clerk-typist, secretary, blue-collar worker, engineer, salesman, management trainee, manager. In other words, a large group of employers seem to be looking for the same general characteristics whether they are hiring filing clerks or marketing managers.

We have no intention of suggesting that any employer would actually evaluate a marketing manager against the same criteria that he uses in filling a rank-and-file job, since the process of filling executive jobs takes place on a different level from the others. Nevertheless, this study stresses something that can be attested to by those who have observed the current process of executive recruitment and selection. The hiring decision seems to rest upon generalized traits (has presence, is aggressive, thinks on his feet, etc.) rather than on a more specific, finely tuned fitting of the man to the realities of the job and the organization.

This often leads to disillusioning mismatches. Just as justice is blind, the process of selecting key managers should be blind to irrelevant superficialities and should probe more deeply into the specifics of the applicant and the position. Indeed we know of one corporate personnel executive who is blind, yet extremely successful. Maybe the fact that he cannot actually see the candidates in front of him enables him to see more deeply into them.

So we have President Jones, favorably impressed by Bob Smith's "presence," leaning toward Smith from the beginning and unconsciously selling Smith on the job. Of course there are other interviews, and others in the firm become involved, but the decision, in the final analysis, is the president's.

Meanwhile what about Smith, the applicant for the managerial post? He has a lot to sell, and he knows it. He is not desperate for a job, he wants to make a change because things have gone stale in his present company. And he is determined that his next job is going to be the right one, one that he can live with. (All next jobs are.) So he should be exceptionally careful about the job he buys. But cosmetic qualities are operating on Smith as well. He senses that Jones likes him, and he is flattered. He is impressed with Jones's presentation of the company's position, its philosophy and its objectives. Moreover, he is convinced that the president is laying it on the line in saying, "I want the right man in this job. If you're that man, you will run your own ship. I believe in giving a good man all the authority and responsibility he can handle—and then letting him go to it." That's good to hear. We all like to think that we will finally wind up in a job where we can call our own shots—even though not all of us are cut out for such jobs, and in spite of the fact that a lot of good men have failed because they worked their way up to spots in which their reach exceeded their grasp.

So Bob Smith begins to want the job. He *knows* that Jones is just the kind of chief executive he can work best for. Here at last he will be able to put it all together and finally do the things he knows he is capable of. Smith is no longer investigating the opportunity, he is waiting and hoping for the offer and doing everything he can to expedite its coming.

What is the job? It doesn't really matter. It's a high executive position that could lie in marketing, or production, or finance. One of the reasons that the actual nature of the job does not matter is that the actual job is discussed in a surprisingly cursory fashion. If the post happens to be that of marketing director, the president satisfies himself that the candidate has a solid background in marketing and that he has a lot of fresh ideas. For his part the applicant discerns the general nature of the assignment. Both men assume that good executive abilities are fully transferable from one organization to another, and in this assumption they are observing the basic tenets of recent management thought.

The inevitable result is that Smith and Jones do get together. They marry in haste, as the old saying has it, and they repent at leisure. Marriage never works out quite the way either of the parties thought it was going to, and the same can be said of the management job. Sometimes it goes better than had been thought, but it often goes much worse.

The manager's success or failure in his new job greatly depends on actions taken by the manager and his new employer in the critical first days—actually even before the new man shows up to take over his duties. This vital initiation period is a subject for another chapter. Now it is time to make some suggestions on how the marriage might have been avoided if it turns out to be a bad match—as well it might, since neither Smith nor Jones has rigorously investigated the actual conditions and circumstances surrounding the new man and his job.

Most job-seeking managers tend to approach decisions vitally affecting their own careers in an unprofessional fashion, one they would certainly never think of adopting in making important decisions within the context of corporate management. An executive meticulously investigates all the factors involved in a plant relocation, yet he is surprisingly ready to relocate himself on the basis of feeling or instinct. He likes the president of the company he has approached. As the younger generation says, the place gives him good vibrations, and he accepts the description of what he will be doing and how he will be doing it at face value.

Why? For one thing, it is hard and troublesome work to really investigate a job offer. If the jobseeker is sold on the idea, he doesn't want to take the chance of letting a good thing slip away. If he appears to scrutinize the offer, or potential offer, too carefully, they may get the feeling that he doesn't really want it.

This is a mistake, and it can be a catastrophic one for the employer, the executive and his family. After all, since the company is thinking of hiring him because of his analytic and decision-making ability as a manager, why shouldn't he use these qualities in providing himself with input for a sound career decision?

He should talk to as many people in the company as he can, his colleagues and even his prospective employees. He should get around the operation, visit other departments, plants, etc. Not surreptitiously. He should ask the top man if it is all right for him to do these things.

If you are in this position, the president—if he is the individual with whom you are dealing—will probably ask why. Your answer is simple. "This is an important decision for both of us, and I want to do everything I can to judge whether or not I can really do a first-rate job for you." Most top executives will not mind this. Why should they? They are more likely to be pleased with a man who looks carefully before he leaps. If the employer does object to reasonable in-house investigation, you may well want to reconsider the firm and the job.

Over and above this, talk to the previous incumbents. Ask who had the job before and find out where he is now. There should be no reason why you should not be entitled to the information. Obviously, in talking to a man who held the job before you, you must be astute in filtering what he has to say, especially if he has been fired. As we said, part of your skill as a manager is to screen information you receive by weighing its intrinsic validity and evaluating its source. If, say, four different men tell you that the job is a dead end and that the president—whatever he says—is not willing to delegate, then you have cause for thought, and an obligation to reopen the subject with the employer and go into it more deeply.

In short, the job-seeking manager should approach the employment decision as he would approach the most important decision he has ever made in his career. To do this he must know himself and what he really wants, he must size up the job opportunity—not with hope but with objectivity—and judge whether or not it really has what he is seeking.

Now let's look at the other side of the coin. When you hire people you are a buyer in the executive emporium. How well you select your people has a commanding influence on how well you function as an executive—and on how much self-realization you derive from your job.

The cardinal point in filling a job is knowing exactly what the job entails. Many managers take for granted that they have this information because the jobholder reports to them. But the organization chart does not guarantee knowledge. All too often an executive does not know what his subordinates do or what problems they face. True, he is familiar with the results that they produce. He can describe the terminus of the route, but he does not know how they get there or what stops they make along the way. Nowadays we tend to manage by results. Objectives are set for subordinates, and the subordinates go away hoping to meet those objectives. In a way this is convenient for the top man. He is supposedly freed from detail and from the obligation of day-to-day supervision. But when it comes time to hire somebody for a job, it is absolutely necessary for him to know more than just what the final performance should look like.

We have talked about the difference between the manager who merely channels the work of subordinates and the manager who actually contributes to that work.

The channeler is at a distinct disadvantage in hiring. He simply does not know what to look for. The contributor —the manager who has worked alongside his people, who has gotten his hands dirty, who has actually performed a multitude of functions—has a feel for the job he is filling.

Use that feel. Encourage the job candidate to talk about how he would solve a specific problem, but don't permit your own knowledge of the function to mislead you. Avoid the pitfall of setting up your own way as a target for the applicant to shoot at. Maybe he has a better way. Listen with an open mind. Use your knowledge of the job to evaluate his method, not to measure it against yours.

The matchup between man and job is one important element of successful hiring, but there is another vital matchup, that between subordinate and boss. You have to live with the man you hire. Can you do that? This is not a question of whether you like him or not. All successful relationships between subordinate and superior are basically job relationships. Personal cordiality and friendship are welcome adjuncts, but they are peripheral to the central problem. Industrial psychologists used to spend a lot of time debating whether it was better for a manager to be task oriented or people oriented. Should his concentration at first be on building rapport with subordinates or on getting the job done? Now most students of management are agreed that this is an artificial distinction. To cite just one study, Dr. Henry Tosi of Michigan State set out to match up workers with, successively, task-oriented and people-oriented managers. Although his assumption was that the workers would like the people-oriented bosses better, he was trying to discover which kind of boss would evoke better performance.

The results did not bear out Dr. Tosi's assumption. Workers not only performed better for the task-oriented managers, they liked them better as well. Other studies have shown that, in fact, there is no such thing as a purely task- or people-oriented manager. Bosses tend to change according to the circumstances.

So the question is not how well you like an applicant, or how much he impresses you with his "presence," but rather how effectively you and he will team up to meet departmental objectives. How much direction will he want from you? To what extent does he really desire a free hand? What will his attitude be when he disagrees with you about something—and what will your attitude be? There is no need to be oblique in approaching these questions. They are too important for elaborate subtlety. Ask him what he expects from a boss in a variety of circumstances. Get him talking about it. Listen, then judge.

When you know the job, and know yourself, you can ask the questions and make the judgments that will lead you to a good working matchup. And you will be penetrating the cosmetic facade that forms the basis for so many ill-considered hiring transactions.

In discussing the selection process at the managerial level we have used the analogy of a marriage. This is apt; two people link themselves in an important relationship. The employer attempts to choose someone whom he can trust and depend on. The applicant must marry not only a boss, but an entire organization.

No matter how many improvements are made in the selection procedure, and even though employer and applicant may really apply sound decision-making judgment to the process, there is still bound to be a high degree of failure. Many newly hired individuals simply do not work out, resulting in disillusionment, frustration, despair, lost time and money, and managerial ineffectiveness.

Why not trial marriages in hiring key executive talent? We believe that the coming years will find industry turning more and more in this direction. A manager is hired on a trial basis, for a period, say, of three months. At the end of that time he and his boss sit down and consider whether or not they will make the arrangement permanent. If either party say no, then the manager leaves. His financial risk is cut, the company agreeing to give him a substantial severance payment, perhaps a year's salary.

When confronted with such a proposal, many chief executives at first are likely to say that it is simply not economically justifiable, that the organization could not afford it. This objection just does not stand examination. It has always been known that it costs an organization a great deal of money, in both direct and indirect costs, when a key executive does not work out and leaves either voluntarily or involuntarily. The company has paid a salary for less-than-adequate performance, and time and profits have been consumed by the manager's lack of effectiveness. In addition, there is the cost of seeking, selecting, and breaking in a replacement.

Within the growing concept of Human Resource Accounting, the first systematic effort to place a viable dollars-and-cents valuation upon the personnel of an organization, there is some interesting work being done in placing measurable values on such occurrences. Dr. Lawrence R. Zeitlin of New York has been active in developing the concept of Human Resource Accounting, and he offers some rule-of-thumb figures. According to Dr. Zeitlin, the overall replacement cost for semiskilled to skilled personnel is half a year's salary; for foremen, supervisors and the lower managerial ranks, it is one year's salary; for policy-level executives, two to three years' salary. At the top levels the figure can become almost astronomical. For example, General Motors estimates the replacement cost for a division head at $2 million—most of it in mistakes while he is learning the job.

So the potential outlay of a year's severance pay after three months on the job may not loom so large compared with the total cost of going much longer with the wrong man, particularly when he will sooner or later have to be replaced anyway. And the cost need not be altogether borne by the company. Many executive search firms offer their client a guarantee, assuring the company that if the candidate who is hired does not pan out within a stated length of time, the search for a replacement will be conducted without additional fee.

Theoretically, a sharp-angling, footloose manager could amass three years' salary in less than a year by cynically entering into such trial agreements. However, even the most rudimentary screening and checking of references would uncover such a scheme.

Trial marriage for managers would give both company and newly hired manager time to size up the relationship and come to intelligent decisions about the wisdom of making it permanent, and it would be extremely likely to upgrade the quality of the break-in period.

In an astonishing number of cases, organizations will hire high-priced and potentially valuable executives and then just permit them to drift through the crucial first weeks. The boss may not be indifferent, he may feel that he should let the new man alone for a while to permit him to get his bearings. Meanwhile the new man may be desperately waiting for some guidance and direction. The result can be a sour start that never permits the relationship to achieve its potential.

The first few weeks on the job are a time of maximum sensitivity to impressions, a period within which a new arrival, who presumably was hired partly because he would bring in some fresh thinking, should be given maximum opportunity to apply that fresh thinking. If nobody pays any attention to him, he will tend, often quite rapidly, to conform, to adopt a protective coloration that makes him look just like everyone else. If it is understood that these vital first weeks are part of a formal trial period, top management is much more likely to pay attention to the new arrival, to appreciate his fresh point of view, and to do everything necessary to make him a fully functioning member of the team as quickly as possible.

It may not be many years before this kind of trial marriage is recognized as a responsible and economical way of hiring key managers. In the meantime, employers and applicants can make the executive job transaction a more rational procedure by going beyond the superficial cosmetic qualities that can be so misleading, by making it a point not to be selling when they should be buying, and by using the full range of management talent and experience to make wise choices in this most important of all decisions.

How to Manage
Success/10

You can find more than a hundred separate listings under business consultant in the Manhattan Yellow Pages. Consultants are paid hundreds of millions annually by American industry, and there are consultants for everything. You can hire a consultant to find you a new president or to tell you what size light bulb you should put in your desk lamp.

The phenomenal growth of the consulting function is generally attributed to the mounting complexity of business, but viewed from another angle, the role of the consultant can be linked with the growing tendency toward professional emasculation of the American manager. According to the well-known Peter Principle, individuals are promoted until they reach their level of incompetence. The Peter Principle may look like a joke, but it is not. The up-or-out pressures in the corporate structure today inevitably put men into responsible positions for which they possess little real experience and perhaps even less native ability. So we have great shoals of executives who, in greater or lesser degree, simply do not know much about what they are supposed to be doing.

This is why the consultant has become a staple of business life. He comes in and does the manager's job or advises about how it should be done, while the manager has been rendered impotent. The consultant, fulfilling the role of a managerial, rather than a sexual, Dr. Masters, comes in and shows him how. Indeed the consultant may be the very person who can cut the mustard when the corporate eunuch is unable to.

Not that the consultant always knows the best way to do the job or to solve the problem. Sometimes he does, sometimes he does not. He has certain procedures that have worked more or less well in a variety of situations. He will size up the situation in a new client organization, apply his standard operating procedures, and couch his report in the most reassuring and authoritative terms.

In many cases the outside consultant supplies considerable help. But in many other cases he offers a kind of magic, a vital element in the lives of our prehistoric ancestors. In *The Golden Bough* Sir James Frazer tells us that "savage man has a . . . conception in which we may detect a germ of the modern notion of natural law or the view of nature as a series of events occurring in an invariable order without the intervention of personal agency." In primitive society the magician was a most important personage. "He appears to have often attained to power by virtue of his supposed proficiency in the black or white art." Our attainment of civilization has not fully eradicated either our natural inclination to believe in magic or our tendency to elevate the role of the magician.

We call these things by different names now. In business the magician may be the consultant. He comes to solve our problems. He possesses his own mysterious rituals and dispenses his black or white art in a mysterious language or symbols. It is often difficult to understand exactly what he is getting at—an approved technique for a magician. Businessmen believe in him and his bag of tricks. They give him money to make things better. And he delivers at least reassurance, if not an improvement. Yet the manager who determines that he will make his way up the corporate ladder, who also realizes that his ascent will inevitably take him farther from the areas of his primary interest and competence, can gain a good deal and learn much from the magicians.

The name of the game in the corporate struggle is promotion or advancement. Dr. Frederick Herzberg places advancement high on his list of motivating factors and adds that advancement is a kind of overall phenomenon that outweighs all the other important motivating factors. "The power of a promotion to increase job satisfaction is often related to feelings of growth, recognition, achievement, responsibility."

Advancement up the lowest rungs of the business ladder may come easily or almost automatically like routine promotions in rank in the armed forces. As the individual moves into the middle and upper management ranks, promotions become not so automatic, and ultimately there comes that one big final promotion, the attainment of which will enable a man to say to himself (even though, as will be seen, it is usually not true), At last I have it made.

Harry Carmichael, sales manager for Leggett Manufacturing, knew for some time that he was approaching that critical point. He had begun with Leggett 15 years back as a sales engineer and had quickly become one of the company's most profitable field men. Moved up to a regional manager's job, Carmichael had turned a marginal region into a high-producing one. His strength lay in his ability to penetrate to the heart of customer problems and to come up with the best solutions.

Carmichael was able to develop that same analytical ability in some of his salesmen, although he was wise enough not to expect it from all of them. With some salesmen Carmichael involved himself thoroughly in the initial stages of major negotiations, with others he managed to instill the kind of drive and resourcefulness that made up for lack of technical know-how.

When the job of sales manager opened up, Harry Carmichael's promotion was natural. He had carved out an enviable record in working with the field force, and there seemed no question that he could apply the same gifts over a wider area.

Carmichael's advancement to the sales manager's position worked out well for him and for Leggett. Of course he was not able to spend as much time with individual salesmen as he had before, but he allocated his time and effort shrewdly and was usually able to be on the spot when needed. His ability to select and evaluate good salesmen, his effectiveness at sizing up tough sales situations, and his inspirational qualities made him a first-rate sales leader.

The next rung up on the ladder at Leggett Manufacturing is vice president of marketing, and about six months before the incumbent VP retired, there were a number of good men in competition for the job. Carmichael of course was one, but Sam Dill, the merchandising and promotion manager, boasted some potent pluses that might make him the company's choice. And then there was the advertising manager, Bert Kelly, young, tough and aggressive, whose influence on marketing policy had quickly spread beyond the confines of advertising.

Besides these candidates, top management might possibly bring somebody in from the outside. Like most firms, Leggett Manufacturing likes to promote from within and prides itself upon being able to do so in most cases. The existence of this policy has been valuable for the firm because it provides a spur to ambitious men. But Leggett had been known to hire from the outside, and Carmichael knew that some good people might be available.

It had been a trying six months. Carmichael pushed himself to the limit to execute certain projects ahead of time. He worked ceaselessly to stay on top of the situation within sales, guarding particularly against the possibility of a major setback, such as the loss of a national account, which would torpedo his chances. On the other hand he had to watch his step. It was important that he make a good showing at high-level meetings, but at the same time Carmichael would not have been human had he not carefully avoided treading on the toes of those who would be making the decision. He was under constant pressure to get around to the branches and yet maintain visibility at corporate headquarters. He was walking a tightrope.

Then there was the strain upon personal relations that was posed by the imminence of the appointment. Harry Carmichael and Sam Dill were friends, and Carmichael also maintained a reasonably cordial relationship with Bert Kelly. They ate lunch with each other, had an occasional drink, played an occasional round of golf, visited each other's house for dinner. But Carmichael sensed the strain that was being placed on the friendship. He and Sam Dill discussed the possibilities of each becoming marketing VP with a certain joviality at first. Each assured the other, "You're the guy I think they are going to go for, and I'll be happy when they do it," but mention of the ever-nearing top-management decision trailed off and finally stopped altogether. Carmichael and Dill continued to see each other, but more and more Carmichael sensed that they were playing charades. With Kelly the atmosphere was even more tense.

The tension was also beginning to tell at home. One night Carmichael's wife said, "Let's face it. I think you deserve the job and they're a bunch of damn ingrates if they don't give it to you. But no matter who gets it I wish to God they would make up their minds. This thing is tearing you apart, Harry. You're crabby, you don't eat. The kids ask me, 'What's the matter with Daddy?'"

When the moment finally came, it was almost anti-climactic. The president of Leggett met Carmichael casually in the corridor and asked him to drop into the office, then he said, "Harry, you of course know that Bill has been wanting to retire to that little farm upstate. Well, I guess the call of the wild has finally been answered. Bill will be going in a month and we'd like you to move in. Of course there will be more money, and we'd like to talk to you about stock. That can be taken care of later. I assume you have somebody in mind for sales manager. Who do you think you'll put in the job?"

And that was that. Carmichael did not telephone home, he preferred to deliver the news in person. Before he left the office for the day, the news was out. Sam Dill came in, a tight smile on his face, and stuck out his hand

103

in congratulations. Dill said the required minimum and left. Watching him go out the door, Carmichael had a strange feeling that he was seeing a friendship end. Bert Kelly's congratulations were even more perfunctory, Kelly adding, "Will you be free tomorrow morning, Harry? There are some plans on the boards that can't wait, and I'd like to fill you in and get your okay." And it dawned on Carmichael that he actually knew very little about what Kelly, and a lot of other people now under his aegis, really did.

Carmichael's wife was relieved and happy, but there was no wild enthusiasm in the Carmichael house. He wondered why he didn't feel better about the whole thing. After all, it was what he had worked for and set his heart on. Now he had made it.

But what had he made?

As the days went on, this feeling grew. Carmichael missed his former warm relationship with Sam Dill. There was no getting around it, that relationship seemed to be gone. Dill was still cordial, but remote in a way that he had never been before. Carmichael told himself, He's disappointed. I'd be, too, if I were in his shoes. But he'll get over it. In his heart, however, Harry Carmichael knew that Dill would not get over it altogether.

What happened to Harry Carmichael happens to a great many managers who finally make it. For one thing, the promotion hangs in the balance for so long it becomes anticlimactic and almost not worth getting when it finally comes. The Bible tells us, "Hope deferred maketh the heart sick." This is a precept that management might well heed in making promotions. When men are vying too long for a specific advancement, the pressure becomes intense. As a result their nerves are stretched to the breaking point, relationships are strained and sometimes shattered, objectivity and effectiveness may suffer markedly.

The feeling of emptiness at having finally made it is only one of Harry Carmichael's worries, for he will find very quickly that you never really make it. The struggle to keep it is intense, and you must almost immediately begin the fight to climb the next rung up the ladder. All too often managers, striving for advancement, breast the tape in front of the pack and then stagger to the side of the track and collapse. They are immobilized by the trauma of success. They wait, delay, get their feet wet, hesitate to move boldly.

Soon top management begins to wonder if it made the right move with Harry. "I thought he had everything going for him when we made the move, but now, I don't know." Inability to function well in a more responsible management job may be partially traced to this trauma of success, but there is another factor that is often at work as well. Consider Harry Carmichael. His record has been built on a particular ability to solve sales problems and to work with salesmen. Now he is thrust into a broader and somewhat alien arena. He must cope with budgeting, advertising policy, long-range planning, finance, and all the rest of it. Harry Carmichael may or may not have the stuff to star in this new arena as he did in the old one, but one thing is sure. He has been removed from sales, the area in which his greatest strengths, and the things he most enjoyed doing, have rested. As a manager working directly with salesmen he was potent and happy. As a high-level marketing executive he may be functionally emasculated, not by his feeling of emptiness at having attained the goal—this will pass away—but by his basic ignorance of some of the adjuncts of his new responsibility.

Sam Dill or Bert Kelly would be at a similar disadvantage. If one were to expect total familiarity with all the functions of higher responsibility, very few people could qualify for promotion. However, this is not the issue. In making it, the manager is often cut off from using the very skills he has so effectively developed, and which he used in a way that brought him fulfillment and satisfaction—self-actualization, in the psychological terms.

One question is, What happens to him as a person now? But another practical question may be more urgent, *How can he learn his new job?* Let's make no mistake about it, most bigger jobs have to be learned. An executive may have perfected a dazzling variety of management techniques in a lower and more restricted position, but this is usually not enough. Most likely, he will soon be faced with something that he knows very little about.

Having made the basic decision, or having had the decision made for him, that he is going all the way on the up-or-out corporate ladder, the manager who gets promoted to a bigger job must learn fast. He must build a record quickly because no matter how much confidence has been placed in him, he is under scrutiny. But an astute manager, placed in the position of a Harry Carmichael, can often resort to magic. He can call upon a magician, that is to say, a consultant, for help in learning his job.

Of course he does not confess that this is what he is doing. We recall the case of one typical manager who was promoted to the top financial job in his company.

This particular man had thought the problem through beforehand. He was well aware that there were certain major functions within the operation with which he was simply not familiar enough. So, a week after receiving the promotion, he put his plan into action.

The manager went to the chief executive officer with a well-constructed proposal that an eminent financial consulting firm be brought in to make a study of the operation and provide some cogent recommendations. "I have some ideas that I think would save us considerable money and give us a much more efficient department," he said, "but I would like some objective third-party input before going ahead."

This proposition made sense to top management. They had used consultants for various purposes, as has almost any company of any size and length of existence. The results of these consultive efforts were not always of the highest quality, but this did not cause any loss of faith in the efficacy of outside consulting as a general rule, because many consultants had actually done a good job. Today the role of the consultant is so firmly established that it would seem almost heretical for a company president to insist that he could do without him. Magic, particularly when it works a fair amount of the time, develops a very strong hold.

So top management agreed to the proposal, and there was general approbation of the newly promoted executive for having made the recommendation. The financial consultants came in, and the manager stuck with them like glue. He followed the consultants around the office, he lunched with them, he plied them with questions, he examined, not just their results, but their methods of coming up with evaluations and proposals.

107

"From these consultants," this manager told us, "I got a crash course in things I desperately needed to know." When the consultants' reports finally came in, he followed some recommendations, ignored others. He had already gotten what he needed—a quick education.

This can be an extremely fast and highly effective way for the upwardly mobile manager to fill in the gaps in his experience. Consultants know their specifications. Their methods are standard and have weathered the test of time. Sometimes their suggestions may not be all that was hoped for, but this need not cast doubt on their general expertise.

If you are determined to keep moving up, you will inevitably attain positions in which you are short of knowledge and experience. It is risky to depend on subordinates to teach you what you need to know. Obviously your instant success may not be the development that is dearest to their hearts.

You can learn from consultants, but it is important to know what you can learn from them. Not judgment, decisiveness, sensitivity or guts, these qualities you must bring to the job yourself. But basic procedures, methods and standard viewpoints, these are the things that the adroit use of consultants can teach you.

Ultimately, of course, you must develop your own expertise and solidify your own particular grasp of the situations that now come within your scope, even though the consulting profession can provide basic training. Given the firm position that the consulting profession occupies in corporate life today, you will be well advised not to ignore a vital educational resource that lies within your power to obtain.

Breaking Through the Confines of the Organization Chart/11

In the normal course of his work, the manager encounters one frustration after another. This is not terribly significant in itself. All of us experience frustration: the housewife, the assembly-line worker, the doctor, the football player, the schoolchild. Frustration is a part of everyday life and the reasonably well-adjusted individual builds up a tolerance to it.

To a considerable extent the executive can balance his frustrations with plus items in his emotional credit column. After all, his position offers him certain enjoyable advantages. He has power, he has status, his job is apt to bring him into the company of congenial and stimulating people, and he is well paid. The money he earns can buy him a comfortable home, freedom from some of the more basic money worries that some people live with constantly, and the option to enjoy himself in leisure moments through swimming, golfing, skiing, traveling, or pursuing exotic and expensive hobbies.

So then why worry about the manager in particular? People in other occupational classes have problems. The very fact that he has status and is paid more money than others often masks the virulence of these difficulties and frustrations, even to himself. Furthermore, there are certain frustrations built into the present-day managerial task that are not found in other occupations to any comparable extent. As we have discussed, one basic factor leading to the emotional emasculation of the manager is his remoteness from the area where things are actually happening. He becomes a channeler rather than a doer, and as a result his sense of accomplishment begins to atrophy.

Serious problems arise. As we have noted, divorce statistics, figures on alcoholism, job-hopping and dropping-out—all expressions of hopelessness and unhappiness—prove this. Small day-to-day frustrations may be offset, or repressed for a while, but the day often comes when their cumulative effect makes itself felt. This is the critical moment when he begins to wonder whether it is all worth it, whether he should not begin to make some waves on his present job, or look around for another job, or even pull out of the rat race altogether. Or he may grit his teeth and try to keep on doing what he has been doing, hoping that things will improve.

When things get worse, he may still keep going with a surface show of self-assurance and satisfaction, but he pays a price in mental and, often, physical health. His wife and children pay a price as well. The critical point may come when an executive is past 40, has hung at about the same level for some years (in the military they call it "overage in grade"), cannot see real possibilities of rising much farther, and feels the pressure from below of younger, ambitious, driving managers. But the climactic moment of frustration need not be deferred until the dangerous forties. It can come at a much earlier stage. And this is happening more frequently, to younger managers, because of the increasing complexity and unsatisfying nature of the executive task.

In such an instance, there is usually one main reason for an eruption of frustration, which is not only distressing in itself but also serves as a focus and catalyst for a whole network of previous disappointments, some going back many years.

Let's examine such a case to illustrate how the blocked executive may find an in-house solution that resolves the problem without endangering his career or violently uprooting him and his family.

Jason Bolton, 34 years old, works for ModernOffice, Inc., an office-furniture company. He came to ModernOffice six years ago as an innovative and effective production man from a competitive office-furniture firm with a good reputation in the industry. Now he is a vice president in charge of the desk and seating division. (ModernOffice also makes conventional and hanging files, storage units of various kinds, and standing and movable partitions.) In his present job, Bolton's responsibility includes not only production but also sales, research and design.

He has moved along fast at ModernOffice and has reason to harbor high expectations. The executive vice president, Max Gramm, is in the middle fifties and has once or twice remarked with some wistfulness on the potential joys of early retirement to the sun and balmy air of Florida. ModernOffice is a closely held family corporation, the chief owner and president, George Grove, is past sixty, and three of Grove's sons are working in the business. None of them seems to have demonstrated anything approaching the father's skill and energy. Bolton is justified in thinking that he might well be the next executive VP and, with some luck, ultimately president and part owner. So Bolton has hope.

In Goethe's words, "There are situations in which hope and fear run together, in which they mutually destroy one another, and lose themselves in a dull indifference." With the increase in Bolton's hope has come an increase in fear, the fear that something will go wrong and ruin the clear picture of advancement that now beckons. As Bolton is well aware, one major mistake or business setback that can be laid at his door will jeopardize his chances severely. He is far from a point of dull indifference, but he is uptight, anxious that nothing of importance go wrong.

And there is danger that something will go wrong. One of ModernOffice's traditionally strong moneymakers has been the A-300 desk, a medium-priced modular line that has built up high acceptance in the trade. While Bolton was running the production end of the desk division, he initiated certain improvements in the A-300 that strengthened its share of the market. Now one of ModernOffice's major competitors, the Clark Company, has made a move that threatens the strong position of the A-300 desk. Clark has installed its own desk line and is aggressively marketing a new type of ball-bearing drawer suspension and file-drawer mechanism that was previously found only in the highest-priced desks. It may be that Clark is not making any money on this innovation, it is a very expensive one for the price that the desk commands, and they have not raised prices. Clark may be using their medium-priced desk as a kind of loss leader to take large dealers away from ModernOffice, but whatever Clark's situation is, the threat is real and immediate.

At first Bolton considered cutting the price on the A-300. After some research and deliberation, he rejected this as a negative move. True, it would save some dealerships, but not the really important ones, and therefore would only defer the day of reckoning rather than solve the problem. Bolton finally decided that the only practical course was to modify the A-300 upward, to install drawer-hanging devices and mechanisms that are competitive with those in use by Clark. But this will not be easy. Bolton's company is in no position to take a profit cut on the line, so the modification will have to result in the A-300 continuing as a strong moneymaker. Bolton figures the pressure of competition will permit some upward movement of prices, but not much.

The improved devices are no problem. They are available, but until now only on ModernOffice's highest-priced lines. The problem affects two areas, production and sales. The new hardware will have to be installed in the A-300 cases at minimum production cost. It will have to be fitted properly within the A-300, which will involve some modification of the case. And the marketing effort will have to be revamped to blunt the thrust of the competitive threat. So Jason Bolton faces a problem that comprises familiar elements in today's management scheme.

In any case the redesigning of the desk went fairly

smoothly, but the production end of his operation is not coming through the way he had hoped. Not only are the modified A-300s costing substantially more as they come off the line, but the new hardware, in many cases, is also not being installed properly. Quality control is turning back an inordinately high number of units. Moreover, faulty units have been shipped, and some weighty customers are unhappy. Bolton is not satisfied with the marketing end either. His sales manager has generated some impressive-looking plans for promotion and presentation of the modified desk, but the salesmen in the field are not selling properly. One reason for this, Bolton concludes, is that they have not been adequately briefed on the technical changes. Liaison between marketing on the one hand and design and production on the other are inadequate.

In attempting to come up with a viable solution to any problem, the manager must first identify and evaluate the major components of the dilemma. Almost always, some of the principal components are people. This case is no exception.

The president, George Grove, stays out of the day-to-day operations of his division managers, but he expects results, and he has a reputation for being quick on the trigger when they are not up to his expectations.

Max Gramm, the executive vice president, is an affable lunchtable companion, but a man who has become increasingly reluctant to go out on any limbs. His remaining active years are limited, he will do nothing to endanger his position at ModernOffice. His influence with George Grove has been and remains high, and subordinates are well aware that Gramm will not act as a shield or an advocate if they get into real trouble.

Gramm is pressing Bolton for results. He has already said, "Jason, it's your baby. You are in this job because you can deliver, and the boss expects the A-300 to ride this out and be an even bigger seller. You have the organization to handle it. Let's see what you can produce."

"You have the organization to handle it." Bolton knows what that means. He has had a reasonably free hand in setting up his division the way he wants, and he cannot now say that he needs a whole new deal. This would not be received kindly. Nor does he want a new deal, but he is having some trouble with the cards which have been dealt to him.

Bolton's key subordinate in this situation is Arthur Carlino, production manager for desks and seating. Bolton groomed Carlino, who is now 29, for his present job. Carlino was Bolton's most valued assistant when Bolton was running production, and assumed the job when Bolton moved up. At the time there was some comment from the top about Carlino's relative youth and lack of experience, but Bolton highly prized the younger man's drive, creativity and imagination. Since then, Bolton feels, his confidence has been borne out. Carlino has introduced some fairly sweeping and impressive changes within his area.

The modification of the A-300 line is the first instance in which Carlino seems to have run into real trouble. Bolton has of course discussed the problem with his subordinate. Carlino, a bright, sensitive, somewhat mercurial young man, has tended to react somewhat touchily. "This is a rough deal that you've handed me, Jason. It's going to take time and work. I've always felt you have the confidence to let me handle the tough ones along with the easy ones. If you don't . . ." Bolton has reassured Carlino of his continuing confidence. Nevertheless, he realizes that his subordinate is having some trouble.

Jason Bolton has gone to the plants, looked over the assembly operations on the desk, and come to some general conclusions which he has shared with Carlino. Bolton itches to do more, to get more actively involved in the day-to-day matter of straightening out the difficulties, but there are factors that militate against his doing this. For one thing, he has a whole division to run, and while the A-300 problem is his most important single challenge at the moment, he cannot drop everything and concentrate on it.

The second factor is Bolton's reluctance to snatch the assignment away from Carlino. Carlino would resent this thoroughly, he is a good man with enormous potential. Bolton knows that such an action on his part would damage the relationship between a key subordinate and himself and that Carlino might well leave. He could get another job, in all likelihood, without too much trouble—and he would be tough to replace.

There is still another factor. Jason Bolton accepts as one of the tenets of good management that the chain of command should not be fractured merely at the whim of the boss. Good executives must delegate. He has implicitly delegated responsibility for these matters to Carlino, and it would be managerially unprofessional to abrogate the bond that has thus been established.

But the temptation to do so is strong. For one thing, Bolton knows the production supervisors on the front line of the A-300 modification project. They represent years of experience, and Bolton wonders if

116

Carlino is tapping that experience to its fullest potential. Bolton remembers that it took him a long time to win the confidence and respect of these skilled supervisors. He knew that this would be one of Carlino's biggest stumbling-blocks, and in this critical period, Bolton wishes that he felt as though the supervisors were coming through with all the help and energy of which they are capable.

One key supervisor is Len Schultz, 47, and with the company for more than 20 years. Schultz's area is critical, it is under his aegis that the new hardware must be fitted into the A-300 cases. Len Schultz is a rough-and-ready type, profane and cynical, but he is highly knowledgeable. His practical savvy could make a big difference at this crucial moment. Bolton has chatted with Schultz on plant visits, and some of the supervisor's passing comments have not been heartening. "Oh, Carlino has it all figured out, with charts and everything. He's a smart boy. Knows all the answers. So let him come up with a way to do it." Bolton thinks, I could get Len's full cooperation, but this would mean by-passing Carlino.

Aside from the negative effect this would have on Carlino, Bolton fears that any such by-passing would cause big trouble. When he was by-passed once, he resented it and thought that it did much more harm than good. So, although Bolton feels that the experience of supervisors like Schultz should be focused more directly on the problem, he is stymied by tradition, a sense of what is managerially fitting, and by the organization chart.

Another key human factor is John Murphy, the man in charge of design in this area. Murphy is 42, a first-rate designer who was once throught of as possessing good potential for moving into a high post in the line organization. But Murphy simply cannot handle people, and so, in Bolton's book, he will be most valuable as a continuing staff operative. Murphy may not agree. He appears to harbor resentment toward Bolton and toward Carlino, resentment that makes itself felt in abrasive comments. Nevertheless, the kind of insight that Murphy has could be useful in solving some of the difficulties involved in turning out the A-300 effectively and economically.

Finally there is the sales manager. This is a somewhat special case for Jason Bolton, for two reasons. For one thing, he would not be looking for contributions from his sales manager in the design and production area. Rather, he feels that the sales manager needs to be brought closer to these functions so that he can do a better job of reshaping the marketing effort on the desk. Secondly the sales manager is somewhat special because he is Paul Grove, the owner's 32-year-old son. Obviously, Paul cannot be fired, or even pushed around too much. Of course, if this were a popular novel like Cameron Hawley's *Executive Suite,* the hero would storm into the owner's office and stake his job and his future with the company on a demand that the son be immediately removed from his job. Things do not so often happen that way in real life.

Paul Grove is by no means a zero quantity. He is smart and is often able to come up with truly startling and useful angles on selling. Besides, he is a likable young man and, in spite of being the owner's son, gets on well with the salesmen. Yet Paul Grove is erratic, he is not an assiduous worker, he has never bothered to learn as much about the manufacturing end as Bolton would like. In this particular case it is a real drawback.

These are the principal human components of the dilemma with which Jason Bolton is grappling. We have mentioned other factors: the pressure from the top for results, the real and volatile threat of competition, the relative rigidity of the organization chart, and Bolton's own well-reasoned reluctance to jeopardize existing relationships to plunge full scale into the A-300 problem.

The situation embodies many of the elements that make life frustrating for executives today. As they reach higher policy-making levels in the organization, they are paradoxically more remote from the arenas in which they have scored their greatest accomplishments. They are precluded by accepted management practice and by the organizational structure from getting their hands dirty and thrusting themselves fully into even the more momentous problems that affect company performance and their own careers. The people who report to them tend to work in sharply defined, highly compartmentalized areas, and when the area of a subordinate seems to be threatened, the territorial imperative comes into play, the subordinate fighting tooth and nail to defend his bailiwick. And yet, over and above all this, performance is demanded.

Bolton experiences his full measure of frustration. He goes home at night wondering if it is all worthwhile. He contemplates the factors that are locking him in. More and more he feels the pressure to cut through the complexities and generate an acceptable solution, and so Bolton finally decides the answer lies in devising a means of bringing all the people involved in the problem, including himself, into a situation in which they can not only communicate and comment but also contribute. This must be done without making startling and disruptive changes in the existing structure. Somehow, to use a term that has come into increasing use among military commanders in Vietnam, an infrastructure must be built, a viable means of attacking the problem within the present structure. In short, a task force.

Jason Bolton acts. He sets up a meeting with Carlino. "Art, I know that you've been working night and day on this thing. And you've done a lot to get it solved, but the hell of it is that a human being has only one head and two hands. I know when I was in your shoes I often wished I could get more help. But the organization has limits."

"It does. Jason, you know we're doing the best we can."

"If you had more help, would you know what to do with it?"

"Sure, but Jason, it would have to be the right kind of help."

"That's right. We can't get any outside consultant, for instance, who is going to be able to come in here and straighten this thing out. But I think there's a way to get you the help you need. From within the shop. I'd like to suggest this for your consideration. Let's cut through departmental lines on this. Let's throw out the chart. I'm suggesting a task force of people whose thinking and direction would make a contribution to your—and our—getting the A-300 shaped up. And I'd like to offer myself as the first volunteer."

Bolton goes on to explain that the task force will be chaired by Carlino. Its membership, without reference to rank or area within the company, will include those who can contribute to the successful implementation of the A-300 project, as well as those who can benefit from a closer relationship with the project. What the task force turns out is designed as input for Carlino, who still makes the salient decisions dictated by his job description. But now, in organized fashion, he is able to call upon a consultative contribution from those who have useful ideas to offer. Moreover, Carlino can request that members of the task force take on specific areas of the general problem. Now, let us face one or two facts. The task-force solution is not a cure-all, not in this case or in any other, nor is a proud and touchy subordinate like Carlino necessarily going to welcome it at first with open arms.

The subordinate does not have any truly logical basis for adamant resistance to the concept, and on reflection, he is likely to see, as in this case Carlino does come to see, that the setup is a rational means of bringing maximum organizational strength to bear on a major problem, without weakening his authority or endangering his future. Substantial contributions can be gotten from people in various kinds of jobs—staff or line, supervisory, managerial or even rank and file—without the attrition that takes place as ideas and recommendations pass up and down through the chain of command, or sideways across departmental barriers. Furthermore, there is a sense of purpose and dedication—of excitement, even—that takes hold when a task force is set up to confront a really major difficulty. True, for many people it is an additional assignment, but by and large, the added work is more than compensated for by the change of pace, the chance to come to grips with a new and important challenge, and the possible opportunity to demonstrate one's ability in a different and perhaps larger sphere.

One of the more attractive features of the task-force approach is its temporary nature. The infrastructure exists only as long as it has a definite purpose; when the job is done, the temporary structure is dismantled. Thus it is not an antagonistic counterpart of the traditional organization, it permits by-passing without resentment or guilt. Another interesting facet to the task-force operation is that it is congenial to a new breed of younger workers, male and female, who want to participate in business, but who bring with them a suspicion and skepticism toward the organization. These people are impatient with old traditions that seem to work to their disadvantage. When the organizational superstructure is swept away, even temporarily, management is able to evoke a fuller measure of the talent and energy that these new workers can provide. And the fact must be faced, businesses that do not take steps to tap this reservoir of different, even difficult, talent are making themselves poor risks for the future.

Most importantly for our purposes, the task-force concept offers the executive who is locked into the confines of managership a way out of his dilemma. By adroit and judicious use of this tool he can set up procedures that enable him to do the things he does best. He can engage in concrete problem-solving situations that help him make a contribution and enjoy the sense of self-fulfillment that this entails. And he can cope with a variety of dilemmas and call upon a broader range of potential contributors without being caught in the toils of "the way we've always done it."

By becoming more of a task-force manager today's

executive can give himself greater freedom and wider scope to get things done. He will feel better about himself while he is doing it. And he can be sure that he is utilizing a technique that will come into increasingly broad use in this changing era of management.

Finally, for many managers this may be an important means of solving the where-am-I-going-and-what-does-it-all-mean syndrome in their present jobs, without embarking on the perilous seas of job change.

Delegate to
Suit Yourself /12

Managers are constantly being told that they do not delegate enough. They hear it from speakers at a variety of conferences. They read it in the standard texts, the more popularized and specialized books on management, and in the business press. Even observers as sophisticated, witty and iconoclastic as Robert Townsend joins the chorus in his best-selling *Up the Organization.* "Many give lip service, but few delegate authority *in important matters. . . .* A real leader . . . delegates as many important matters as he can because that creates a climate in which people grow."

The development of subordinates is one of the two basic reasons for increased delegation, the other is managerial efficiency. Auren Uris, in *Developing Your Executive Skills,* expresses the prevailing viewpoint: "Delegation is a sanity saver for several reasons. It gives you freedom of action, allowing you to turn your attention to the areas of your job that need it most. It gives you more time to spend on long-range planning.

"But greater efficiency isn't the only reason for dele-

gating a part of your job. Enlargement of a subordinate's job can give three other important results:

Developing his sense of responsibility
Enlarging his general understanding
Increasing his job satisfaction."

These are worthy objectives. Managers should be as
effective as they can be, and subordinates should be
developed within a climate of maximum job satisfaction.
Now let's take a closer look at the realities of the
climate within which an executive faces the hard decision whether to delegate or not to delegate. If he is
conscientious and abreast of his profession, the typical
manager is aware that a great many eminent and authoritative people are telling him to delegate more. He
feels that he is doing things that subordinates should be
doing, and not just trivial things, important ones. Peter
Drucker has remarked that "every manager does many
things that are not managing": analyzing the market,
designing a plant, negotiating financial arrangements,
and so forth. When an executive does these things, it is
very likely that he does them well, but still he is told
that they are not part of the job of management and
that the sooner he arranges for a subordinate to do
them, the better off he will be.
Consider yourself as a manager. There are, no
doubt, particular skills that you acquired and applied
earlier in your career. If you are a marketing man, you
may have developed a special strategic sense that en-
abled you to carry an intricate transaction through the
maze of a large national account and finally bring it to

fruition. If you are a production man, you may have developed the ability to look at an assembly operation and spot instantly the slight duplication of effort that was leading to the loss of valuable time. Now that you have moved on to bigger things, must you stop doing what you can do so superbly and delegate it to a subordinate? Most current thinking on delegation would urge you to do so. You may be inclined to delegate the parts of the job that are irksome and keep the parts that are fun, but this does not accord with standard advice. Indeed, Townsend says, "A real leader does as much dog-work for his people as he can," and farms out the really important and exciting tasks.

The idea, of course, is that in having others do even the more important and exciting tasks, you are freeing yourself to do the things that a manager is really supposed to do. Planning is usually suggested as the prime example of what the properly delegating executive is freeing himself for.

This does not always work out so well in practice. We talked with the president of a large manufacturing company who had come to the top from the sales area. In his earlier days he had been known as a tenacious and inspired salesman, competitive against even the heaviest odds, and in his selling and marketing days, he had been a stickler for detail. His principle was that even the most insignificant thing might make or break the deal. Arriving at the presidency, this man continued to involve himself in important top-level sales negotiations, at least for a time. Then several of his key managers confronted him. They pointed out that the president was not delegating properly, that they should be given more responsibility and more freedom to handle their ends of the business. The top man should concentrate on long-range planning. The confrontation had its effect. The president became a scrupulous delegator. It was painful, but he conditioned himself to keep his nose out of the operations of those reporting to him. He tried to concern himself with planning and the big picture.

Not long ago this president said, "I sit here in this office and I feel like the Prisoner of Zenda. My top men do their jobs well. I have no serious complaints about any of them. But every now and then I see something that I know I could handle better if I dove into it. But I can't dive in. I can talk to a man, make suggestions, but I can't just go in and do it. It wouldn't be fair to him. They tell me that I should spend my time planning, but after a while just thinking about the future gets kind of boring. And besides, how can I plan when I don't have a first-hand feel for what is going on, on the firing line?"

He has a couple of points. Planning is important, but should a high-level executive be forced to spend most of his time doing it because he has risen above the problem-solving level? And isn't there a serious danger that when a manager is too far removed from day-to-day operation, planning may become an abstract and unrealistic exercise?

John D. Rockefeller senior flourished before the days management was developed into the science that it is today. Perhaps that is why he never felt compelled to keep his nose out of the details of lower-level operations. There are numerous anecdotes attesting to this. For example, one day Mr. Rockefeller was being taken on a tour of a refinery. At one work station he was shown a worker swiftly nailing tops onto barrels. The plant manager commented proudly, "He uses exactly twenty nails on each barrel." They moved on, but the oil magnate was preoccupied. Finally he asked, "Could he do it with eighteen nails?" As you may readily imagine, they tried it with eighteen nails. That didn't work, but it was found that nineteen nails did work. Just one man and one nail, but when multiplied throughout the operation, the time saved was considerable. Old John D. was not the most sparkling personality in corporate history, but nobody ever said he did not know how to run a business.

When a manager has a specialty that he can perform better than anyone else, it seems wasteful to us to require him to stop applying that special knowledge or skill in the name of delegation. Carl Hovgard is the founder and now retired president of Research Institute of America, which produces printed advice for businessmen in a variety of areas. Carl Hovgard is a gifted man in many respects. One of his strengths is an instinctive ability to judge how a publication should look so that its content have maximum impact and sales effectiveness.

Before his retirement Hovgard was surrounded by editorial specialists who were highly competent at researching and writing the company's material, but who were not necessarily adept at format and packaging. One day, during a coffee break at a Research Institute meeting, the president approached one of his editorial department heads and asked, "Why do you still use that brown ink on the cornercards of your envelopes? It's terrible." It so happened that the subject of the previous session —conducted by an eminent professor of business administration—had been delegation. The editor replied,

"Carl, don't you think you should at least delegate the color of the cornercards?" And Hovgard responded mildly and rather wistfully, "I've been delegating that for ten years, but nobody has yet done what I want!"

The editor had his own standing and self-image to consider. The cornercards remained brown. Perhaps it might be worthwhile to speculate whether the president, who knew more about this detail of the business than anyone else, should have been obliged to refrain from seeing that the right thing was done just because he was president.

Similarly, managers frequently avoid doing things they can do better than subordinates, because the principles of delegation dictate that they must keep hands off. When this happens, the organization loses the use of a valuable skill, and we wonder if the traditionally cited benefits of delegation always make up for it.

This is not the only problem. One of the reasons cited for increased delegation is the enhancement of job satisfaction for the subordinate, but when a manager stops doing the things that he does best and the things that are fun (they are fun because he does them well), what happens to his own job satisfaction? There are situations in which the executive may find that he has delegated himself into sterility. Many times this is an important element in bringing on the restless, anxious feeling that the job does not offer the rewards that it used to. Of course it doesn't. Even though money and status have increased, it has become a less satisfying job.

It might be said that the manager who really likes doing something is not likely to give it up, but the realities of business life do not bear this out. For one thing, there is always pressure to delegate more, not only from the standard sources of accepted management practice but also from within the organization as well. The subordinate pushes for greater responsibility, with the implied threat that he will go elsewhere if he is not granted it. And the boss pushes his key managers to delegate more: they should not be bogged down in detail, they should be developing their own replacements.

Yet it is inaccurate to conceive of the typical manager as holding all the reins in his hand and being free to delegate or not delegate as he pleases. Delegation is frequently implicit in the way an organization works, it is built into the organization chart. This is particularly true when a manager takes over a new operation. His predecessor has probably delegated in a way peculiar to his own style and in his own accommodation to what he thinks of as the dictates of the manager's job, and these ventures in delegation have become part and parcel of the way the division works. The newcomer simply cannot overturn the machinery and lay out a completely new pattern of delegated responsibility. There would be chaos, people would rebel. So he accepts the pattern, perhaps thinking that he will change things gradually, but this often proves extremely difficult.

Overdelegation—and the wrong kind of delegation —can emasculate a manager professionally. If he assigns the lion's share of important activities to subordinates, he puts himself in a passive position, and as George S. Odiorne observes, management is not a passive art. What can be done about delegation? How can you arrange matters so that you are not bogged down in detail and your subordinates have scope for self-development and job satisfaction, and yet still be able to do what you do best and enjoy most?

Start with the parts of your job that you find most burdensome. Robert Townsend would have you not delegate the dog-work, but we do not agree. What is dog-work to you may be interesting to someone else. Furthermore, it is unlikely that you are superlative at things you don't enjoy doing. So do farm out the dog-work. Don't let the subordinate gauge the extent to which you are glad to get rid of it, but then, don't pretend that the assignment is a particularly scintillating one. Lay it out as it is, a job that has to be done. Set up standards that should be met and discuss general principles for getting the job done. Listen to the subordinate, let him have his head. He shouldn't do it the way you do. His different approach is apt to be at least as good as yours, and probably better. He will be developing problem-solving abilities that you already possess, and you will be freed of some draining, dispiriting chores.

Next we come to the middle classification. These are responsibilities that you handle reasonably well and do not find particularly irksome. In delegating them, emphasize the opportunity and challenge that the act of delegation affords the subordinate, but don't feel, in every case, that you must make a complete and final break with the responsibility and forever after hold your peace. Some experts insist that it must be done this way, but that proposition does not prove out in practice.

Gradual delegation is frequently a better method. Gradual delegation means that you do not release all of the strings on the project at once. The subordinate may be impatient with this, as might be expected. Any ambitious individual has some need to feel that he can take over any assignment lock, stock and barrel. If you have clearly outlined that he will take on a greater portion of the assignment until his responsibility is complete, the subordinate can live with it.

In many cases, although the subordinate may not admit it, he will be glad to live with it. As management consultant Spencer Stuart comments, the strings attached to a delegated responsibility may constitute safety lines for the person on the receiving end of the delegation. It is useful to remember that wanting more responsibility does not automatically assure that responsibility can be handled or that it will even be welcome when it arrives suddenly and completely. Graduality in delegation is simple enough to set up, once the manager accepts the principle. It just means the establishment of checkpoints (they might be called fail-safe points) at which manager and subordinate review what has been done and discuss what must be done next. As the delegation proceeds satisfactorily, the intervals between the checkpoints are increased until finally the delegated job rests completely in the hands of the subordinate.

Lastly we come to the labors of love, the elements of the job that the manager really handles well and enjoys doing. Don't be too quick to delegate these. After all, your prime responsibility is not to delegate, or even to build strong subordinates. Your principal function is performance, both short and long term. Everything that you do about organizing your own job and the jobs of subordinates is focused on this broad objective. You must weigh your superiority in performing a certain function against the long-range benefit of developing

132

somebody else to do it. But weighing the matter need not dictate instant delegation. Your special skill may be paramount in assuring short-term high performance, and without a good short term there may not be a long term.

There is a further consideration here. Planning and thinking about the big picture are things that any executive must do, but he needs an inflow of realistic information to plan and think intelligently. Your rate of inflow is a function of your grasp on what is actually happening. If you divorce yourself too completely from the hard facts of present reality, your capacity as a planner is considerably diminished. So you have to retain contact with day-to-day operations. Looking at reports of what has already happened does not provide this. The most effective way for a manager to maintain this necessary contact is by doing what he does best.

It follows then, that if you are to be a contributing manager and not just a channeler of the efforts of others, an active participant and not just a passive evaluator, you have to do things. Doing the things you enjoy and excel at is not self-indulgence, it keeps you in trim and makes you a better manager. So think carefully before delegating away an important specialty. You need not keep it all to yourself. Let key subordinates in on the act, discuss it with them, call upon their assistance, demonstrate your method of operation as a training device, but keep the final say in your own hands.

What about the situation in which your objective judgment tells you that the time has come to delegate a prized activity, one in which you are at your best? Then by all means delegate, but in this instance you may want to consider delegation on an in-house consultant basis. This means that you turn the job over to a subordinate with the proviso that you are to be considered as a consulting resource. Emphasize that this is implicit in the transaction. Some subordinates may not be too happy with such an arrangement, but if you have truly mastered the function, there is no logical basis upon which they can argue against it. As an in-house consultant, you are still in touch with the project and have reasonable freedom to give your skills some profitable exercise. You will not have delegated yourself into an empty corner in which you brood about the lack of satisfaction in your job. Delegation is a valuable management tool, but it is just that, a tool and not a commandment. The way you delegate should support your function as a contributing manager, not supersede it.

The Problem of
Visibility/13

Caught in a frustrating situation, the manager can do many things to alter his job and make it more rewarding and satisfying, but let's face it, this does not always work. When all the avenues for change within the present framework are blocked, the question becomes, What now? and the answer of course is, Move. Either drop off the management merry-go-round altogether or move on to another job. Most executives prefer the latter and less extreme alternative.

You, or any other manager, can go out and look for a job on your own, but in today's business world that usually is not the way it's done. Rather, the job comes seeking the man. Some managers seem to be lucky this way, and to those of us who are less lucky, these executives seem to be constantly sought out by job opportunities. They are asked to lunch by executive search professionals, they are approached directly or indirectly by top management at other companies.

When we compare the character, abilities and track record of one manager, who is often sought after, against those of another, who never gets an offer, there is often no clear indication of what makes the difference. Naturally, if you are in the unfortunate position of the man who does not get the offers, it's hard to be objective about this. But even when the question is studied objectively, it often turns out that the man who is not approached has it all over the man who is approached.

Bad luck, we might say. But let's examine that kind of luck a little more carefully. When we do we are apt to find that it isn't luck at all.

Let's cite a typical case. Two managers, Edmund Foster and Larry Koenig, work at marketing headquarters for a large manufacturing corporation. Both have good, responsible jobs and both have demonstrated considerable talent and character. Ed Foster, who is 34 to Larry Koenig's 32, has been with the company a little longer, makes a little more money, carries a little more responsibility. If you were to take a poll of the two men's colleagues within the organization, the edge would go to Foster. Larry Koenig is able enough, but Ed Foster has something special in the way of capacity. He is a sound, solid, level-headed performer. He is never flustered by problems or pressures. He is honest and fair, people like him and trust him, and he has guts. When he decides what is right, he stands up for his convictions in a quiet, logical, reasonable way. Foster does not flaunt his resoluteness. He exerts it only when it is called for.

On the other hand, Larry Koenig is quick, intuitive, fast-moving. He likes to talk and to bounce his ideas off others. Koenig is more outgoing than Foster, who talks cogently and to the point when it is necessary. Larry Koenig is a great collector and exchanger of ideas, many of them offbeat. His gregariousness and search for creative ideas take him on trips around the country and out of it to a variety of conferences, meetings, conventions. Once Koenig returned from a three-day session and Foster asked him what he had gotten out of it. The younger man replied, "It was a bomb. Not even a single halfway decent notion in the whole three days." Foster just shook his head and smiled, he doesn't like to waste time like that. He has seen Koenig in action at meetings and he knows that Koenig usually contributes far more than he takes away. Foster prefers to save his energies for the manifold problems he meets every day on the job.

Although they are unlike each other in many ways, the two men are friends. They discuss their feelings and their hangups, Koenig openly and volubly, Foster with a little more reticence. For some time they have been discussing a difficulty that they share. Each is unhappy with certain aspects of top-management policy. They have tried to effect changes but have been frustrated more often than not. Both have shared the growing conviction that perhaps it is time to leave.

Ed Foster has begun to make an effort to find another job, but he has been running into trouble. His best qualities are not apparent at first glance (we previously discussed the importance of cosmetics in the job interview). Foster has been approached, obliquely, by the president of a smaller company in the same industry. There is a job there, but Foster wonders if it is the right job for him. He wishes that the setup in the other company were different, that he liked it better. Otherwise, he has been putting feelers out, but it is slow going.

Larry Koenig, on the other hand, does not face this problem. At the moment he is considering three job possibilities, all of which were initiated by someone else. In two cases, the first contact was made by an executive searcher. In the third, the feeler came from the company itself. One organization is in the same industry, two are in different lines of enterprise. Koenig is in the process of weighing, picking and choosing. Over the lunchtable, he tells his friend Ed Foster about his progress. Foster is pleased, but being human he cannot help being a little envious and puzzled. I'm at least as good a man as Larry, he says to himself. And indeed an objective observer would rate him a better man, but it is Larry Koenig who is being approached and who is being offered the opportunities and the money.

Why? The answer is visibility. There is a constant search for good managerial talent, but the hunters cannot seek a man out if they can't see him. Larry Koenig is visible and, to a number of organizations, highly desirable. Ed Foster is an excellent executive and would be a considerable asset to many companies, but these companies—and the professionals they retain to seek out talent—simply do not know that Foster is there.

Career visibility has always been a problem for the executive who wants to succeed and grow. It's worse today than it has ever been. Business has become huge and impersonal. A man isn't Tom or Dick or Harry or Ed anymore, he's a name in a box on an organization chart. Sometimes he's just a number.

As a safeguard against stagnation and frustration, today's executive must have potential mobility. Ideally he should be in a position to consider other job offers at any given time. Many managers enjoy this happy state of affairs, but others as good, or better, become as defeated in the process of job-hunting as they are on their present jobs, so they stay where they are and become more frustrated, more boxed in, more disheartened, more embittered.

How can you achieve the kind of corporate visibility that makes you a man who is sought after? How can you be the kind of manager who, when an executive search firm is looking for somebody to fill a larger and more responsible job, receives an invitation to lunch to talk over some possibilities? The business world is not going to move heaven and earth to seek you out. You must be easy to spot.

Max Gunther, the writer and commentator on the business world, tells of a convention of the American Chemical Society that he covered a few years ago. One obscure young delegate at the convention discarded his official name tag in favor of an enormous yellow cardboard disc which he had designed and made himself and which carried his name, degrees and company name in vivid red. Throughout the convention the young delegate was seen in earnest conversation with different groups of older man. At one point, having ascertained who Gunther was, this chemist approached him and said, "Here is a list of subjects that I am up on. Any time you're doing a story where you would need quotes on these topics, give me a call." The young man went on to describe how for six years he had been working quietly and loyally for a large company. He felt lost in the shuffle; management did not seem to know that he existed. So the chemist had determined to do something about it. When the opportunity came along for him to attend the convention, he said, "Now or never."

Six months later Gunther needed clarification on some aspect of a story he was doing for a magazine.

Remembering the aggressive young chemist and his affiliation, he placed a phone call. The chemist was gone. An older colleague explained, perhaps with some hint of acerbity, that "a hustling little outfit snapped him up and now he's second in command of their new European operation. It was odd, you know. He was a shy kid, sat around here for years and never said boo. Suddenly he's making more noise than a brass band . . . but it does make you feel strange being left behind that fast."

By a single act of personal determination the young chemist had become visible, and being visible, it was only a matter of time until he was sought out and given the opportunity to move up to something better. Those who are invisible are left behind, and they often wonder why it happened to them. As one job counselor puts it, "The question isn't how many men are available, it's how many men are visible." Herbert Imhoff, president and board chairman of a Chicago-based search firm says, "There's a growing shortage of senior executives. By 1975, this country will need 1.7 million managers. The opportunities in coming years will be enormous, but if a man wants to be a part of this, he must step forward and tell people who he is."

Favorable visibility is not a matter of luck. If you want opportunity to come to you, rather than the other way around, you must make yourself seen not only by the right people outside your organization but also by top management within the organization as well. The opportunities are there, but if you cannot be seen, they will go to those who are more visible.

In analyzing this achieving of visibility, let's look at the ways in which executive recruiters—head hunters —find talent. You may be a needle in a haystack, but if you are a shinier, more prominent needle than the others, then the talent seekers will find you out. Here is the basic manual of visibility techniques.

Membership in professional societies. The search for an executive to fill a particular spot often begins with a perusal of a society's membership list. For example, Battalia, Lotz was retained to find an executive to head up a new Bunker Ramo Corporation division. The kind of man who could take on this responsibility was likely to be a member of the Association for Computing Machinery. We wrote letters to the members of the society and began our search that way. After a considerable process of evaluating and narrowing down the list, Bunker Ramo eventually hired one of those who turned up in the very first batch. True, some associations are far more active than others, and the meetings of some of them can be a deadly bore for the manager with an active mind. Nevertheless, your name on such a list enhances your visibility, and your membership enhances your possibilities for useful contacts and other visibility-heightening activities.

Writing articles for professional journals. The executive who reaches an audience of his colleagues through the medium of print is apt to be considered a man with initiative and ideas. When your name appears as author of an article, you are doing more than conveying information to your peers or to the wider business world. You are saying, in effect, I am a man with something to contribute. For example, we were given an assignment to find a chemical engineer of a highly specialized breed. We combed through industry magazines and sought out men who had written articles on particular subjects. The man who was finally tapped for the important job had written his article years ago—reluctantly, as a favor to the journal's editor—and had thus become visible in the process.

Many managers have thoughts that would be welcomed as contributions by periodicals, but they think, "I am not a good professional writer, nor do I have time to write." This is simply not a viable objection these days. Ghost-writing is no longer the exclusive province of politicians or candidates for master's degrees. Many alert and ambitious executives have found that with a little effort a reasonably skillful writer can be located to do the work of putting the manager's thoughts into publishable form. The ghost writer will frequently be a writer from a public relations job, a house-organ editor, or a newspaper or magazine staff editor. There are always writers looking for extra work, and they watch the classified ads.

A personal press program. Some people seem to get their names in the newspapers frequently and are often being quoted by trade magazines. This does not just happen. Writers and editors look for people who can be reached and quoted on topics of reader interest. This gives variety and texture to their articles. Moreover, they are looking for news, and what they print is read by leaders in industry and search professionals. To take a typical example, one executive, upon his promotion to a new post, took the trouble to send out a press release describing the promotion and adding a brief autobiography. This was printed as a matter of routine in a trade periodical. The announcement came to the attention of a head hunter, and the result was a new job for the executive at $8,000 more per year.

Maintaining ties with former colleagues. Out of

sight, out of mind is a poor formula for successful visibility. The people with whom you have worked can provide a potentially influential and ever-growing network along whose lines opportunities and job offers may come back to you. One fast-moving executive has made a point of keeping in touch with every one of his old bosses after moving on to a new job. We were looking for a manager to fill an extremely important position, and one of this executive's former bosses recommended him. We looked him up. We liked him, the company liked him. He got the job. It was that simple.

Attending conventions. We have already talked about the marked visibility achieved by the young chemist at an industry conference. While this man went all out, his experience is not by any means isolated. Any given conference is a pig in a poke as far as substance is concerned, but being there and meeting people is an excellent step toward favorable visibility. Head hunters usually attend conferences where they're apt to meet likely candidates. Beyond that, the people who meet you and remember you at a convention may one day be instrumental in getting you that better job which will bring true self-fulfillment.

Panelism. More and more educational institutions look toward the business and management community for help in providing their students with diversified fare. One middle-aged executive we know was shy. He never did much of anything about putting himself forward and obtaining the kind of visibility that would give him the kinds of opportunities he merited. Yet he was talked into sitting on a panel in a midwestern university. The subjects discussed were why some college students think business is irrelevant and what businessmen should do about it. It was not an earthshaking session, nor did it achieve any particular prominence, but it was written up in an alumni magazine. Six months later an executive search man happened upon the report of the panel's deliberations. He was looking for a manager in this executive's skill area. The search man and his client liked the executive's ideas, and as it turned out, they liked him. He is now a happier man in a much better job.

Civic activism. From time to time most executives find themselves pressured from one source or another to become more active in the community. Often the temptation is to say, Well, I put in enough time and energy on the job. I'm better off relaxing and playing golf or boating.

Civic activism can provide useful visibility in some surprising ways. One manager agreed, without enthusiasm, to accompany his son on a weekend Boy Scout camping trip. There he met another executive who had been similarly dragooned into making the trip and they got to exchanging ideas about business. We were looking for a candidate. We telephoned the second man. "That's an odd coincidence," he said, "I was talking to an impressive fellow on a camping trip just the other night."

The school board, the community chest, the hospital board of directors, the planning or zoning board, all can provide satisfaction and favorable visibility.

Keeping in touch with executive search organizations. Reputable search firms work on assignment. They do not deal in bodies, but at the same time they maintain files on promising managers who may possibly fit a future search. One manager kept in touch with Battalia, Lotz by writing at least once a year keeping his file up to date. His specialty is fairly narrow, and jobs that would be

144

suitable for him just do not come along. But finally one did. A medical foundation was looking for a particular kind of man—and our correspondent filled the bill.

Many richly endowed executives are quite modest. Some are indeed shy. You, like them, may dislike blowing your own horn, but this natural reticence must be weighed against your responsibilities to yourself and to your family in terms of your career. When you express your confidence in your own ideas and ability to others, you are not puffing yourself up. You are indulging in natural pride that is part and parcel of the makeup of any good manager. Naturally, no executive should engage in visibility-enhancing activities that are absolute agony to him, but perhaps the agony of being stuck in an unrewarding and frustrating job can be far worse. Some small steps taken now to begin a corporate visibility program can assure you of wider opportunity, career fulfillment and a more satisfying and healthy life.

Playing the
Corporate Field/14

"If only I had. . ." The manager who comes to a dead end in his career feels that he does not have much left, but he has his memories. Unfortunately, these memories are wistful, regretful, self-accusatory. If he has moved from job to job, there is always one company he wishes he had stayed with. If on the other hand he has stayed with one organization, he now castigates himself for not having taken one or more of the big opportunities that came his way. None of this looking back is of much use now.

The manager who is still young enough to make some substantial decisions about his career can reverse the process and project himself 15 years into the future. What kind of a career pattern will he be looking back on? He may be looking back from the crest of success or the trough of failure, there is no way to tell. But there is one thing that the manager can do. He can make decisions now that will assure that when he looks back over his life he will be seeing a pattern chosen by him, not a random course over which he drifted because of chance and the breaks.

In a way, the young manager can eat his cake and have it too. He can sow his managerial wild oats, give himself a fair shot at making it to the top of a greasy pole, and at the same time prepare a fallback position for himself if he should fall in the climb. This involves making clear-cut and momentous career decisions at an early stage. They cannot be avoided or deferred for very long.

Your career decisions are made whether you make them or not. If you do not make the decisions for yourself, they will be made for you by other people and by outside circumstances. Let's say you get a job offer in another city, but your wife says that it would be very inconvenient to move. Or you suddenly leave your present company, where things have been going pretty well for you, because you have had a fight with your boss and another offer happened to come along at the critical time. Perhaps you accept transfer to another assignment which you do not feel comfortable about but which you take because top management asks and it just doesn't seem possible to turn them down.

Whatever you do, whichever way you turn, there is no way to assure yourself a successful career, but you can do things which will assure you that wherever you are in 15 years, you will be there more or less as a result of your own deliberate strategy and your own will. With some preparation, a manager can have two careers. During his first, he can give it everything he's got in a valiant effort to reach the top in the corporate struggle, but somewhere in the back of his mind should be the thought that he may not make it, and at least a general answer to the question, What do I do then? If, before it is too late, the executive considers his situation objectively and concludes that the continuing struggle upward is not worth it, he may have a second and perhaps more satisfying career on a plateau of safety. That second career on the same plateau we will consider elsewhere in this book, but now let's consider that first career.

As the writer Max Gunther observes in *True*, there are two broad areas of strategy. One is choosing the career style that is right for you, the other is knowing how to manage that career style. The term *career style* can have a lot of ramifications, but in a basic sense it comes down to this question, Will you get married to the company or will you play the field? Some men make it to the top by staying with one outfit. Others range from job to job and wind up in the seat of power.

Gunther cites two capsule case histories of success, each in a different career style. A. Clark Daugherty chose company wedlock as a career style. He joined the Rockwell Manufacturing Company as a sales trainee right after college and stayed there. At the age of 40, Daugherty became president of the company.

The career style of Dave Phillips is job-hopping. Until Phillips joined the State Farm Insurance Companies in his mid-30s, he had never been with one organization more than three and a half years. On some jobs he had stayed no more than one year. But shuttling between jobs kept him moving upward until he took over as an assistant vice president of State Farm with a large salary and a wide-open road to the top.

Some men find that company wedlock becomes a dismal, lifelong, no-escape situation. They have had opportunities to move early but have not taken them. Later the opportunities dwindle and finally stop. The manager is stuck in a dead-end job beyond which he will not rise and in which he becomes less and less secure as the pressure from below increases.

The job-hopper on the other hand might find that his last hop has bounced him into a dead end. The first job changes are to significantly better positions, but later on he hops for little gain in compensation or opportunity. Finally he reaches a point at which there are very few places left to which to move and none of which offers any particular promise. Indeed, as top management regards this job-hopper's checkered résumé, he may have considerable difficulty in finding a spot at all.

The goal is the presidency. Within each organization there is a track that leads to that goal. The young manager must be able to distinguish that track. It is not always clearly marked; often the pointers are obscure. It is a matter of intuition, of feel. One fairly standard indicator may be found by looking at the kind of men who have made it to the top in a particular organization. Where have they come from? Sales? Production? Manufacturing? Engineering? What kind of people are they? Bold? Careful? Quiet? Domineering? The manager must be able to develop a profile of success in his present organization and size himself up objectively against that profile. If there are glaring lacks, or if he feels that he would be straining uncomfortably to fit certain aspects of the profile, it may be that he is not on the presidential track and will never be on it.

There is another important question, Who up there likes you? The ambitious manager does not seek out a patron in the sense of a Renaissance artist seeking the favor of a Lorenzo de Medici, but if his work does not catch the eye and win the approval of the real influentials in the firm, he must face the fact that things are apt to get tougher, not easier as time goes on.

When a man is not on the presidential track, the mere hopping to another job may not be of any help. He must pick his spot, he must do everything possible to obtain at least a rough idea of the track to the pinnacle in the prospective organization, and once again judge whether he has what it takes there.

The decision on the right career style should be made early, probably by the time a man is 30, a further judgment whether he has managed his career style properly should be made not much later than 40. In general, 40 is the age when the really big jobs begin to open up for the man who has handled himself correctly. If this is not happening, then it may be time to think seriously about settling for the second, safer, less arduous career.

Which career style, company wedlock or job-hopping, seems to offer the most promise? In a study made by the American Institute of Management, 200 presidents were picked at random, their biographies examined, and the number of companies each president has worked for was tabulated. Here are the results:

48.5% had worked for one company
21.2% had worked for two companies
14.7% had worked for three companies
8.3% had worked for four companies
2.0% had worked for five companies
5.3% had worked for six or more companies

Obviously company wedlock is the surer road to success. This seems particularly true when the above results are compared with those of a similar survey conducted by AIM 17 years before. Of 200 presidents analyzed then:

36.5% had worked for one company
19.5% had worked for two companies
17.6% had worked for three companies
6.9% had worked for four companies
4.4% had worked for five companies
15.1% had worked for six or more companies

The strong implication is that success is most assured to the man who gets on the presidential track within one organization and stays there. He may have to move to another company, he may even have to make two moves, but once he is on the track he should stick with it. Of course it must be noted that there are certain industries—advertising for one—where the contrary is true. Here, job-hopping is the accepted way of moving to the top. In such an industry, the man who stays more than a few years at one organization is suspected of being an unimaginative plodder.

Perhaps more important than the particular career style that a man chooses is his manner of managing that career style. Let's look at it from the point of view of the executive search man. Assume that the search man is seeking an over-$30,000 a year engineering executive for a medium-sized electronics company. He is considering two men. Both happen to be molded into the company-wedlock career pattern.

Executive A is 49 and has been with his company 22 years. For the past 8 years he has been supervising a production process at a small plant. He is earning

$16,000. Executive B is 46. He has been with his company 23 years and has been promoted at least once every three years. For the last two years he has supervised all production at a large plant. He now makes $27,000 a year.

Executive A has done it wrong. Obviously he reached a plateau early in his career. From then on he has apparently been satisfied with getting an automatic $500 a year raise. He should have job-hopped when he hit that plateau, but he didn't. Why? There could be a number of reasons. He might be afraid of change. He might be unsure of himself. He might be unwilling to meet new people and new situations. Whatever the reason or combination of reasons, he does not look like a good bet for the job to be filled.

Executive B, on the other hand, looks good. He has stayed with the same company, but he has not stagnated. If he ever hit a plateau, he pushed himself off it quickly. He has moved along and stacks up as a man with a future. On paper, which is the way a lot of these things are judged, he looks like a better bet.

Now let's assume that the executive search man is also seeking to fill a marketing job. He is looking at the résumés of two job-hoppers. Each is in his early 40s. Each started as an industrial-equipment salesman and hopped his way up to a job in which he now oversees the work of other salesmen.

One man has worked for 12 companies in his 20-year career and is now earning about $20,000. He has hopped regularly every one or two years. The second man has worked for eight companies. He hopped often while in his 20s and early 30s, but he has held his previous job four years and his present one six years. He is earning $32,000. The first man is in trouble. The search professional assumes that his first job might have paid him $5,000. This means he has hopped 11 times to get raised by $15,000, a little more than $1,000 each time. He hops for small, quick raises instead of big raises and real personal growth. Now he's in a trap. No company will hire this man for a bigger job than he has. A prospective employer will think, What's the use of hiring him and breaking him in? Somebody else will offer him a lousy $1,000 a year more and he'll be gone.

The second man is in good shape. No longer does anyone hold it against a man if he job-hops often while young. If he hops more slowly as he gets older and more sure of himself, his record gives the impression of increasing stability. Furthermore, his record on paper projects the image of personal growth. His more recent job moves have been for considerable salary increases, and the assumption is that they have involved much more responsibility. This man seems to be worth hiring.

The question of whether to wed or to hop is an individual one. Many factors are woven into every man's job and every job change. Job situations can go sour through no fault of the man in them. In such a case he is a fool if he does not hop. Success requires more than just a set of rules. You have to tune those rules to your own situation, using your own wits.

Most important of all, whether a manager stays wedded to a company or plays the field, he must always have an objective view of himself and of his progress upward in the corporate struggle. When he begins to look as if he is hanging in the stretch, he must face that truth and confess to himself that he may not have it for the long pull. This involves an agonizing reappraisal of the rest of his life. If it is conducted early enough, he still has time to shift his whole style of working and living over into another area, one that provides him with satisfaction on the job, a decent income and a happier, less pressure-filled existence.

The Search for the Safe Plateau/15

Darwin presented to the world a picture of the struggle for evolutionary survival that was red in fang and claw. The corporate struggle is bloodless, but it can be ferocious. And the effects upon its casualties can be devastating.

Here is a typical story of one such casualty. Walter Cartwright joined Mohican Inc. twelve years ago as a personnel assistant. Within a few years he became recognized as a first-rate employment man. He was skillful at drawing up job descriptions, adept at selection of test batteries that would really predict performance on the job, easygoing and yet penetrating as an interviewer, and reliable as an evaluator of applicants.

Cartwright liked employment work, and still does. He is sure of himself as he works through all the steps of recruitment, evaluation, selection and hiring. He realizes the importance of the function and has received gratifying accolades from line managers who have come to rely heavily on his judgment. As his experience and grasp of his craft have increased, he has been able to introduce certain innovations in employment practice that have gotten him recognition outside the confines of Mohican Inc. (One new departure in interviewing technique was reported fairly widely in personnel journals.)

All this time Cartwright worked for the amiable and competent Francis Kelly, personnel manager for Mohican. Kelly had at one time been a line executive in the production area, but, although extremely well liked by the top brass at Mohican, he was no ball of fire, and as new technology brought new demands in production, he had become a problem for top management. Nobody wanted to get rid of good old Fran Kelly, but something had to be done. So they gave him the personnel job, reasoning, as is so often the case, that he gets along well with people.

Kelly's transfer from line to staff worked out better than a lot of such moves do. He developed reasonable ability at personnel work, which was not considered to be exactly a cosmically big deal at Mohican, at least at that time, and he was smart enough to recognize a good assistant when he found one in Walter Cartwright. At last the time came when Francis Kelly's tenure was about to come to an end. Not one to hang in the job until he dropped, Kelly indicated that early retirement would be all right with him. There was no great sentiment at the top to persuade him to remain.

In the meantime Mohican has grown. The work force is four times what it was when Fran Kelly took over, and double what it was when Walter Cartwright moved into the employment job. And top management has come to think of personnel as a much more important function than they ever did before. To a considerable extent this has been due to the efforts of Cartwright.

Walter Cartwright has zealously and enthusiastically

promoted the human development vital for the corporation of today and tomorrow. He has foreseen that this function would fill an increasingly important role at Mohican. For years Cartwright has been preparing himself for his move up the corporate ladder, the key move, as he sees it, of his career. Knowing that employment, no matter how good a man may be at it, is only one part of the overall personnel function, he has worked hard to equip himself with all the armament necessary for a top corporate job in his field. He has struggled to give himself facility in training, corporate development, manpower planning, wage and hour administration, labor relations, communications, and all the rest of the paraphernalia of a vice president of personnel for a leading corporation.

That is how Cartwright sees it, vice president of personnel, with direct access to the president. As Kelly's date of retirement begins to draw near, Cartwright has every reason to believe that top management also sees it that way. With Kelly as the incumbent, the title and status of the job has not been elevated beyond personnel director, and Kelly's place in the corporate hierarchy has remained a relatively subordinate one, with the department reporting to a vice president for administration.

Soon, Walter Cartwright believes, all that is going to change. His days of self-schooling, his arduous trips to seminars, his nights of study, are going to pay off. There are strong indications that the organization chart will be changed to upgrade the function when Kelly retires. Kelly himself, in his humorously wry way, has told his young and ambitious assistant that the top brass has "gotten religion" about personnel. Fran Kelly himself does not give much of a damn, he has never lusted for power, being content to remain at a relatively low station in the Mohican setup, "out of the zone of fire," as he puts it. Walter Cartwright has always liked Kelly, but he would not be honest if he did not admit to himself that he has been somewhat scornful and impatient at the older man's lack of ambition. The manpower function needs and deserves full professional representation in the high executive quarters, and this will surely come about under Cartwright, for Walter Cartwright has received what he considers to be oblique assurances that the job of vice president of personnel will be created, and he has every reason to assume that he will fill it. After all, who else?

When the climactic day comes about a week before Kelly's last scheduled day, Cartwright is called to a meeting in the president's office for what he senses will be the big announcement. "Walt," the president begins, "you have done a great deal to convince us of the importance of a stronger, more forward-looking personnel function here, one that swings the right amount of weight in policy matters. We think you're right. What we do about people now will determine how this company goes in the next ten years. So we're creating the position of vice president of personnel. All functions relating to manpower will come under him. He will report directly to me, and he will sit on the policy committee."

Walter Cartwright tries to maintain a sober and attentive mien, but inwardly, he is singing, he is jubilant. This is it: Slowly he picks up the thread of the president's words, "And of course we realize that some of your really outstanding capabilities have not had full scope to develop. To a good extent that is our fault, because of our slowness to recognize some of the developments taking place in your area, but you will certainly have ample scope now. We've considered very carefully who would be the most experienced and best possible man to handle this job. We had a thorough search made, and I think you'll agree that we came up with an outstanding man. Monday, Jim Barkus, who was VP for corporate development at Acme and whom I'm sure you've heard a lot about, will be coming in to take over as vice president of personnel for us. And with you as his right-hand man—and he is looking forward to working with you—we expect before long that we will have a personnel operation that is second to none in this industry."

There is more of this, but Cartwright's mind is such a seething jumble that he can hardly take it in. Somehow he gets through the interview with the president and stumbles out. He doesn't know if he has been tactful or said the right things, and he doesn't give a damn. Everything has collapsed around him.

When this happens, and it happens to a lot of executives, the victim is subject to a number of reactions, many of them simultaneous.

Rage. He is terribly angry. He would like to assault, or at least see something horrible happen, to the boss who conveys the decision and the lucky, even if innocent, man who gets the job he wanted.

Stupefaction. He is stunned. His mental processes are numbed, and this state may continue for some time.

Self-reproach. He wonders, What's the matter with me? What did I do wrong? Did I think I had it so sewed up that I coasted? Maybe he did, it would be natural.

Resentment. His resentment—I'll show that SOB!— grows out of his initial rage and can last a long time. It would be pleasant to assume, as many managers comfortably do, that this feeling is translated into positive effort to do an even better job, but often this is not the case. Resentment at not receiving what was due may lead to an indifferent performance, even to unconscious and sometimes even conscious sabotage.

Despair. I've had it! the victim cries to himself. All those years and all that effort wasted. What do I do now?

Apathy. This can be the final stage. Who gives a damn? the manager wonders and does not try anymore. The vicissitudes of corporate life have effectively emasculated him.

Determination. Many men fight off apathy and instead determine to plow ahead, in the offending company or in another one, to achieve the recognition and advancement that has been denied. This reaction, the determination to succeed next time, is the reaction that is traditionally approved by those who speak and write about how to win success.

Determination is what conventional wisdom dictates that Walter Cartwright must display. Above all things, he must not accept defeat. On the other hand he must not sulk, he must not be a poor loser. What Cartwright has to do, according to the American corporate success story, is to throw himself with renewed effort into the fray and at last climb to the heights he has designated as his goal, and so there are two roads for Cartwright, one of which he must choose. On the one hand he can remain at Mohican, continuing to impress top management with his credentials until they at last see the light and give him the power and status that he deserves. (What happens to Barkus, the new man in the job? Well, that's another story.) The other positive alternative for Cartwright—and for the many thousands who have found themselves in Cartwright's position—is to go elsewhere, get another job. Of course the other job must be a step up, with more money, a more resounding title, and at least a portion of the power and responsibility that he tried for in his previous job. If Cartwright does this, he becomes another chapter in the continuing story of management success.

In this respect the management success story is like that of the successful politician who rises to great heights upon the stepping stones of past defeats. Perhaps this kind of success reaches its zenith in the story of Richard Nixon, whose ascent to the top of what Disraeli called the greasy pole climaxed numerous defeats and humiliations. In his book *Six Crises*, Mr. Nixon gives the rationale for this kind of struggle. "What counts is whether the individual used what chances he had. Did he risk all when the stakes were such that he might win or lose all? Did he affirmatively seek the opportunities to use his talents to the utmost in causes that went beyond personal and family considerations?" In Mr. Nixon's view, only if a man is willing to take this kind of risk for himself and others can he truly find himself. At the end, a man must answer the question, "Did I live up to my capabilities as fully as I could? Or were only part of my abilities ever called into action?" Good questions. But they are not the only questions, and we submit that they are not the most appropriate questions.

Let's look at Walter Cartwright again. It may be that Cartwright has been trying to live up to his capabilities as fully as he could, but all too often the situation is different. Driven by the *machismo* of success, an executive tries to live up to capabilities that he does not

161

possess. Walter Cartwright is an excellent employment man. He likes the work and he does it well. Why should he spend so much time trying to make himself into an expert, or at least a plausible performer, in labor relations, corporate development, and all the rest of it?

The obvious answer is to get ahead. If a man does not broaden himself, prepare himself to handle a bigger job and a wider range of challenges, he cannot get ahead. Get ahead—*to where?* Realistically it may be that Walter Cartwright is not a vice president, but only an employment manager. Tradition says that he will never find out unless he tries, and that a man who does not aspire to bigger things is not ambitious. And although Brutus found ambition to be a significant drawback to his cordial relationship with Julius Caesar, it is a quality much prized by those who hire executives. In fact, it is difficult to think of cases in management recruitment in which ambition is not explicitly stated or tacitly understood as a requirement.

Why is ambition so important? Is it not conceivable that a man who is dedicated to his work, who enjoys doing it, and who does it well, will be of far more value to the organization than the ambitious individual who is constantly looking upward? Which is more important, the length of a man's stride or the number of patters his shoes make on the floor? Let's make no mistake about it, ambition is not a quality that assures zealous attention to the job at hand. When a man's eyes are always cast upward it may sometimes be a little hard for him to see what he is doing. If we could translate the organization charts of many companies into pictures of the men in the boxes, we would find each box occupied by a fellow who is eyeing the next box above his.

In a way this is all right. Everyone is looking up, so all have an equal advantage or handicap. When ambition is the norm, there is no way for top management to accurately gauge the contribution that might be made by a man who is not ambitious in that sense. But the organization might be a lot better off if ambition were not accepted uncritically as a desirable trait. Nevertheless, it is. And so it must be considered a fact of life. This does not mean that a man must fall into a bottomless abyss if he drops, either inadvertently or by choice, off the greasy pole.

Walter Cartwright might try to hang in there at Mohican and prove that he is a better bet for vice president than the man who actually got the job, but it must be assumed that Jim Barkus, who got the job, is not an utter fool. If Cartwright's ambition becomes too naked and too dangerous, he is through at Mohican. That truth is not always added to the injunction that a man must always strive ambitiously upward.

Suppose Cartwright does look around and finally gets another job, one with more responsibility. When he does this, the slope becomes steeper. He is away from the turf he has grown to know so well and on which he made his record. He may or may not be able to handle the increased responsibility, but he will certainly be doing less of what he is really skilled at and what he really enjoys.

Let's suggest another road for Walter Cartwright. He can stay at Mohican. He can do everything he can to help, and become invaluable to, the new vice president. He can stick to being a superb employment manager and carve out such a permanent niche that his position as an asset to the company will never be questioned. He will get raises, receive deserved accolades, become a professional paragon at his specialty. He will get home at regular hours, enjoy vacations when they are scheduled, spend time with his wife and his growing family. But he will probably never be vice president. And it is from this aspect of the scenario that the average management man recoils. Cartwright would be abdicating his ambition, and there is something unseemly, even unmanly, in that.

Is this the case? We do not think so. We think that the safe plateau is the best answer for a vast number of the Walter Cartwrights in the corporate world. Moreover, we submit that organizations would function more effectively if more thought were given to providing safe plateaus to skilled and enthusiastic men, rather than requiring them to continue to fight their way upwards toward what, in the Peter Principle, is justly called their level of incompetence. The manager who seeks the safe plateau is, of course, not exhibiting the kind of risk-it-all courage that is particularly extolled by those who have already made it. He is going against the grain of the American Dream, and he is acting like that most reprehensible of characters, a quitter.

Yes, the man who drops out of the desperate struggle upward is a quitter. He is quitting a life of tension and crisis that exacts a price not only from the individual himself, who after all, has made at least a tacit decision to pay it, but also from his wife and his children, who were not told of the dangerous shoals when they signed on for the cruise.

Moving to the safe plateau may be accomplished in a number of ways. It may involve the move from line to staff, an activity which goes against the impulse that dictates that the guy with real guts and ambition should move from staff to line, where the real action is. It may mean remaining in the line, but perfecting a unique skill that makes its possessor a recognized asset to the organization. It may be that the manager who wants to go this route will have to create the plateau for himself because no such job presently exists within the seething wolfpack of ambitious strivers. There can be a measure of office politics attached to the move, but the man who makes it may find it desirable to attach himself to a higher-level, potentially successful striver to whom he is a great asset but no threat. We will look at all of these possibilities, but basically, before the move to safety is made, the manager must make a fundamental decision. He must review his situation, look down the slope of the rest of his life, and tell himself what he wants to get out of his continuing corporate career. If he chooses to become a conscientious objector in the battle for corporate supremacy, then we say there is every reason for that to be considered an honorable decision. More than that, the man who chooses this road can be an extremely valuable and fully realized person. He can do a job he does well, and have fun doing it. Attaining the presidency of ITT might be nice, but even if we all had what it takes, the job can be held by only one man at a time. Life holds other rewards.

How to Win
by Losing/16

If you make up your mind to do something, if you carefully plan how you are going to do it, if you carry out your plan against all of the obstacles which you encounter, then it can be done. There will be times when you think it is hopeless. You will be lonely sometimes, feeling that there is no one that you can talk to. There will be moments when you'll think you have been very foolish to ever embark on this course, but stick to your plan and you can carry it out.

The foregoing may sound like a typical generalized excerpt from one of the numerous books and articles that tell you how to climb the ladder, how to achieve the topmost goals of your management career, how to succeed. But this is not a treatise on how the winning of friends and the influencing of people, or the power of positive thinking, can make you chairman of the board. Our purpose here is to offer some working guidelines, not on how to succeed, but on how to drop out of the success spiral. In other words, this chapter is about how to quit successfully.

We are not talking about quitting your job. We are not talking about withdrawing from life. We are talking about a reordering of priorities in which a manager looks ahead and looks around him—and decides that continued striving upward is no longer going to be the most important thing in his life.

While the majority of managers do drop out of the success spiral, the trouble is that in all too many cases, they leave it grudgingly, unwillingly, miserably and at the most inopportune moment. We are suggesting that instead of waiting until calamity strikes, managers should make the withdrawal willingly, rationally and at the right time.

Of course we have been fed on success stories, and quitting goes against the American grain. Yet, in truth, there is very little room at the top. A man may believe he has the ability to make it, but ability is far from being the only requirement. More than merit is required. It takes luck, a considerable measure of ruthlessness, and a few dedicated neuroses. Even if the ultimate goal were certain, it might not be worth the price, but since ultimate success is far from a certainty, and indeed extremely remote, the manager must ask himself if the continued struggle is worth what he, his wife and his family will be asked to pay.

If you are still going all out for advancement, perhaps it is time to take an inventory of your situation. This is worthwhile no matter how old you are or no matter how far up the ladder you have climbed. It may be particularly critical for those who are reaching or who have passed the critical age of 40.

The kind of inventory we are talking about is not

167

quantitative. It is not a count of cases or units or amounts. It is objective, a great deal depends on how you do things and how you feel about them.

For example, how do you feel about your job? Do you approach it with the zest of earlier days? For many managers the task of administration becomes pure drudgery. They do not fully realize that they are miserable on the job, or if they do realize it, they shrug and continue to try to bear the frustrations and tensions. Indeed, as we have remarked, a lot of management men confer status upon themselves by becoming proud of their hangups. As Erich Fromm observed, we boast about our neuroses because they are after all peculiarly our own. This is eminently true at certain management levels.

How do you feel about the people who report to you? David Ogilvy once said that when he came to work some days, all the people around him struck him as fledgling birds with their mouths open and waiting to be fed. There is no getting away from it, the higher a manager goes, the more emotional mouths he has to feed among those who are beneath him. At first his responsibility can be extremely stimulating. Some managers feel good about it throughout their careers, but others find the situation more and more burdensome until it is virtually insupportable. When a subordinate looms up in your office doorway with a piece of paper in his hand, are you eager to tackle his problem or do you wish to God that he would go away? A reasonably objective inventory of such reactions can help determine the degree to which your job is still fun.

Are you still moving upward at a satisfactory pace? Or do you notice others who seem to be moving faster?

In particular, do you feel pushed from below? The young can be very heartless. Right now a lot of executives are having one or two drinks too many and one or two hours of sleep too few because they feel the pressure from younger, more aggressive competitors. If this seems to be happening, your mind and your body are merely responding to a natural process. You can fight, but what an enormous toll the struggle will take from you.

How is everything at home? Do you commute back and forth between arenas of tension? Do you and your wife talk, have fun, do things together? Is sex still one of the free, natural joys of married life or are there increasing constraints imposed by emotional exhaustion, disinterest, and perhaps fear of nonperformance. Are your children a pleasure or are they increasingly alien beings who seem to stare contemptuously at what you are and what you stand for? Today's children with their outspoken arrogance and their unwillingness to accept the old values provide a particularly piercing headache for a good many executives caught in the spiral road to success. The kids are disobedient, uncooperative and contemptuous. They want help and support, but they are not nice about it. You can't reason with them, you can't transfer them, and you can't fire them.

As you take your self-inventory, it may begin to appear that the odds on ultimate, complete success are stacked far against you. But whatever the odds, assume that in the end you make it all, money, power, prestige, the whole bit. Will it really have been worthwhile? What will you really have?

Many managers answer, "Not enough," but they can see no reasonable alternative. After all, they reason,

I have to make a living. Yet there is an alternative—and one that is considerably short of the extreme of dropping out altogether. It is possible to drop out of the upward spiral and still make a decent living and live an eminently satisfactory life working at things that you enjoy and do well. If a manager has made the basic decision that this is what he wants to do, it is possible for him to begin a new kind of life in his present company, his present job situation.

Of course the decision must be made, and with it the manager must accept a whole new set of priorities. He must discard the goals that once seemed important and replace them with new ones.

Let's say that you have made the basic decision to drop out of the quest for the Bitch Goddess Success and seek the safe plateau. How can you begin to do this?

Focus on your personal area of unique competence. Professor David Ewing of the Harvard School of Business points out that at the lower level of management, the individual acquires problem-solving skills. In the classic progression, the higher he goes the less important these skills are to him and he becomes much more concerned with broad-gauge policy and planning skills.

In thinking about your own problem-solving stage at an earlier point in your career or in your present job, look for the one thing or set of related things that you did best and enjoyed doing most. For the personnel man, this might constitute the area of employment. The marketing vice president may have been best at, and gotten the greatest kicks from, working through complex negotiated sales with large national accounts. The production executive may have starred at the reorganization of assembly-line setups for maximum output, and so on.

Locate a function which you did well and which you liked doing. It may well be that a considerable measure of your advancement is based upon your facility in this area, and as you have attained greater responsibility, you have felt compelled to turn your back on it and involve yourself more with administration and long-range planning. Go back to your specialty. Get involved with it again.

In a sense, anyone can administer and plan, and it may be a long time before results disclose that a certain individual was not a very good administrator or planner after all. But solving important problems does get immediate results and provide immediate satisfaction. True, as our view of the top-level manager is presently constituted, it does not equip you to become chairman of the board, but remember, you have already made a basic decision. You are seeking the safe plateau.

Become invaluable to a man who is going to make it. The fact that, in your heart, you have made the decision to drop out of the desperate race for the top gives you certain advantages. With eyes less clouded by ambition and envy, you can look around you and above you and gauge who is likely to make it. Pick a winner. Then having made your choice, set out to place your unique problem-solving skills at the winner's disposal. By your actions make it clear that you are not a rival but rather a resource and a support. In developing your problem-solving skill in a particular area, you are moving toward a position of unique importance. You are becoming stronger at an important function which your colleagues are ignoring. You are building muscles which they are permitting to lapse into obsolescence.

Become the trusted advisor. The demarcation between line and staff is far less sharp than it used to be. With the advent of the task-force approach, line men perform staff functions. Conversely there are staff men who no longer fit the traditional concept of the person who serves in an advisory capacity but does not really make decisions. They are given authority, they have clout. By developing your area of unique expertise, if it is important and well chosen, you may well find your problem-solving ability called into play in a broader and broader arena. True, you will be working at the behest of other men, but this is the role that you have chosen.

Ultimately you will find that you have escaped the gravitational pull of ambition. You will have given up what may well have been the extremely illusory chance to become president of the company. But you will have gained a great measure of security. You will enjoy what you are doing and feel better when you go home at night. You will be more than adequately compensated because you can do certain things that nobody else can do.

In the end, you will probably be a more productive and valuable individual than the manager who does make it to the rarefied environs of top-most managerial responsibility, only to find that he lives with paper work, frustration and increasing despair for what seems 25 hours a day.

Manager, Manage Thyself/17

In *Think,* a biography of the Watsons and IBM, William Rodgers writes that the favorite phrase of T. Vincent Learson of IBM, when he was talking about a manager who had not met a project schedule, was, "I'll cut his balls off."

Mr. Learson, we hope and assume, was speaking figuratively. But figurative emasculation can be just as painful, dreadful and ultimately fatal as the genuine article, it just takes longer. And a lot of managers are undergoing the awful process, not at the hands of bosses, even such dynamic ones as Mr. Learson, but through the slow grinding of the system into which millions, from the Learsons to the newest executive trainees, are trying to fit as components.

For these managers, there was a time when every day was bright with promise; the feeling of power and responsibility was exhilarating; money, status and privilege did good things for the body and soul. As the years stretched on, the satisfactions began to lose zest, there were occasional and then more frequent spasms of sharp pain, and underlying all, a dull ache, at first almost imperceptible. Why have they permitted themselves to endure this progressively unrewarding existence? The answers vary, but they boil down to this: these things are all part of a management career.

If most executives managed their business interests the way they manage their own career problems, the corporate rate of failure would be astronomical. Inevitably, from global giants to mom-and-pop grocery stores, bad and even catastrophic business errors are being made every day. But the people responsible for these erroneous decisions are making them from what they at least conceive to be hardheaded decisions.

They have amassed relevant data and looked at the situation objectively. They have arrayed the various alternatives before them and examined them closely. They have projected the consequences of every possible decision into the future. They have genuinely attempted to work out plans that lead toward growth and profit, and they certainly have tried to avoid the disastrous consequences of early drifting along in a Micawberish fantasy that something will turn up.

Since we are all fallible, the most effective planning and the most incisive decisions are sometimes just not successful. When was the last time an Edsel pulled up alongside you at a traffic light? But, in business, managers strive to apply knowledge, experience, skill and insight to the problems with which they are grappling. They know that businesses are not run on vague hopes, Utopian dreams or baseless hunches. Most management operations are based on a cold-eyed appraisal of the real-world situation, and when wrong decisions are made, the error is finally faced head on.

At heart quite a few managers who fancy themselves cold-eyed realists are incurable romantics. Sure, they laugh at the simplistic notion that, by pluck and luck, a red-blooded American boy can always see it through and make his way to the top, but they handle their affairs as if this proposition were scientific fact or even Holy Writ. And so we have the picture of managers who are able to operate with great efficiency in the office while permitting their personal lives to flounder into calamity.

One of those whe sees this picture over and over again is Dr. Charles P. Neumann, medical director of Silver Hill Foundation, a private psychiatric hospital in the gold coast town of New Canaan, Connecticut. Silver Hill's patient list, according to New York *Sunday News* reporter Patricia McCormack, includes "more and more corporate executives who are alcoholics." Dr. Neumann views many of his patients as victims of the legacy left by the sainted Horatio Alger. "Case after case illustrates how affluence and high position are no buffer against feelings of inadequacy, dependency problems, anxiety, depression, loneliness, rage, repressed sexuality and the multiplicity of dynamics evident in the drinking of upper-class alcoholics." Dr. Neumann's patients are not business failures. They are business successes.

Upper-level alcoholism is only one indication that we may well be in a paradoxical bind, that success in a management career may bring one to the brink of failure in life. There are other indications that this may be the case: the divorce statistics, the rebellion of children against the values and ethics of their elders, the deterioration of national mental health, the spirit of unease and unhappiness abroad in the land.

For years the manager has been exhorted to take

stock of himself periodically and make firm decisions about his career. Business literature is full of such urgings, but somehow they don't take. Perhaps the typical manager is an eternal optimist who has formed the habit of always expecting eventual success. Or perhaps, as Antony Jay sets forth in his recent book *Corporation Man,* managers are driven onward by primal urges that constitute the heritage of their apelike ancestors of millions of years ago.

Mr. Jay's book is an interesting example of the current tendency to apply the New Biology to human behavior by extrapolating upward from the behavior of lower animals. Such advocates of the new science as Konrad Lorenz, Robert Ardrey, Desmond Morris and Lionel Tiger look at the behavior of birds, fish and mammals and then transfer to man the workings of such phenomena as aggresssion, mock combat, the territorial imperative, male bonding, and so forth. As a matter of fact, the analogy between business and the conduct of lower animals has long been featured in advice to career-builders. Books with titles like *How to Survive in the Corporate Jungle* abound on the executive shelves.

Is it really a jungle? In fighting our way up through the organization chart, are we merely playing out some primeval pattern embedded in our genes from time immemorial? If this is the case, then maybe there is little we can do except to struggle along the career path, regardless of the cost to ourselves and to those who are close to us.

We don't believe that this is the case. We are not fully masters of our fate, but we have far more potential mastery than we are using. Too often we abdicate that mastery to pursue something called success.

Is success something worth striving after? The problem is one of definition. If we consider success to be a seat on the board of directors, then by definition a great many are instantly excluded from the possibility of success. But if success means a decent, happy and productive life, then it is possible for all to achieve it.

It is not enough to suggest that a manager should use his skills to manage his career better. Rather he should bring all of his resources to bear on managing his life better. For a lot of men this might mean they stop thinking about their careers (they may no longer have careers) and start thinking about making a living. When the manager gives up his dream of occupying the president's chair, he can open up a whole new range of possibilities for himself. He can see things he has not seen for years, enjoy things he has not enjoyed, come back to life as a human being. He does not have to drop out in the sense of becoming a long-haired hippie, he can still do a job and take home a paycheck, and frequently he will enjoy it more. All he will have dropped out of is the frantic race to the top.

The time for the stay-in-or-drop-out decision comes to every management man. Tragically, many don't know when it has come. Yet the decision is always made, although it is frequently made by omission, the manager opting to stay in the losing race because he cannot conceive of doing otherwise. In this book we have tried to suggest how he can do otherwise—and make a success of it.

The career/life decision begins with self-evaluation. The decision is not an easy one to make, it is not even an easy one to face, but the realistic manager should anticipate having to make it. A lot depends upon how well he decides.

How much fun is he getting out of what he does for a living? Fun? Yes. When you bring the question up this way with some executives, they are apt to look at you oddly. After all, who says that business is supposed to be fun? But on the other hand, why shouldn't it be? You don't have to call it fun, call it motivation, satisfaction, self-realization, that indefinable something that nourishes the soul.

Every manager should take a fun-on-the-job, self-inventory. The sooner the better. How has your job changed? Very likely you are making more money than when you started out, you have more prestige and more power, but are the kicks still there? Do you like things you do now as well as those you did before? Do you worry more? Or less? When you go home at night can you point to specific things you did during the day and say, "I did that and I feel good about it"?

This is not to suggest that work at the middle and upper management levels should be a barrel of laughs. It can and usually does involve a great deal of strain and tension. Some people thrive on tension. It sets the adrenalin flowing and arouses them for the big challenges. The most successful managers like tough problems, they like not just overcoming them but also the rigorous inner sweat and turmoil involved in their solutions.

Some psychologists are too ready to write off things like money and status as hygiene factors which provide no real motivation. One executive put it to us this way,

"Do I like being a division manager? Frankly, I often find it a pain in the ass. In many ways I was happier when I was out on the line. But when I go home I have a swimming pool, a boat, a workshop and the best set of golf clubs that money can buy. I eat well, I drink well and I drive damn good cars. My wife looks good to me because she spends a lot of money on looking good. Call me a materialist, I don't care. I have these things and I enjoy them and I want to keep them. And this can keep me going through the dullest three-hour meeting."

So, in evaluating the fun that he derives from his job, the manager should take into account all aspects of it. He must give full weight to the extent to which he is able to enjoy the things that money can buy. And who doesn't enjoy prestige and power? It is very pleasant to have people defer to you, and it can be a substantial, if little-admitted, thrill to realize that people are afraid of you.

But self-evaluation is only part of the inventory. It is also important to take a look ahead at the rest of your life, both on and off the job, and to develop the basis for some decisions. In that regard it is useful to go back and review the sources of on-the-job satisfactions with one paramount question in mind, How long can they last? The "tiger," who gets a fierce enjoyment out of the rugged corporate struggle, will find that the organs do not pump up the adrenalin quite so readily as he gets older. The man whose principal satisfactions come from the privileges of success—money, prestige, power—will realize that the provision of these benefits never stabilizes. He cannot stay in one place, he must keep moving up. The atmosphere can be delightful on the higher reaches of the greasy pole, but when you stop climbing, you may slide down.

If after a reasonably objective appraisal, the manager concludes that his greatest satisfaction comes out of doing a particular kind of task or solving a particular kind of problem, then he must face the realization that continued success will take him farther and farther away from his forte and element. Of course he can console himself that there will be trade-offs. He may find himself doing things that he likes less, but then there is the money, the prestige, the joys of recognition and achievement. Well, those benefits may lie ahead, but there is no guarantee. A manager must ask himself if the struggle to achieve them is really worthwhile, if their realization, when and if achieved, can really make up for the absence of the things he likes best.

There is no formula for significant self-appraisal in the context of career and life. It is just a matter of thinking—really thinking—about yourself and bringing some modicum of managerial ability to bear on the distinct and urgent problem of achieving a successful life.